The Long Season

The
Long
Season

ONE YEAR OF BICYCLE ROAD RACING IN CALIFORNIA

Bruno Schull

BREAKAWAY BOOKS
HALCOTTSVILLE, NEW YORK
2002

The Long Season: One Year of Bicycle Road Racing in California

Copyright © 2002 by Bruno Schull

ISBN: 1-891369-32-6

Library of Congress Control Number: 2002109912

Published by Breakaway Books
P.O. Box 24
Halcottsville, NY 12438
(800) 548-4348
www.breakawaybooks.com

FIFTH PRINTING

NOVEMBER 2003

"People tell me that I express the emotions of the peloton and explain exactly why things happen during a race. I think this is because I was only an average rider and not a champion. I know how hard cycling really is."
—Davide Cassani, former professional bicycle racer

W e came over the headlands and down toward the water on the road that followed the side of the hills. I sat up on the bicycle and watched the pack spread out in the early morning sun. The front stretched into a long line around the corners, and you could see the bicycles and riders and bright jerseys moving against the country, and the blue water coming closer as we descended. Gradually the road ran out on the flats and we came back together into the large group, reached the coast, and turned north along the water.

It was the first road race of the 1995 season. I settled into the steady even pace, looking ahead down the long California coast toward the massed brown headlands and yellow cliffs. Behind there were the smooth rolling hills and the land sweeping up to the ridge of mountains that ran parallel to the water. Along the road were stands of trees and white beaches, and farther out black rocks and the flat shining Pacific. Mist was rising from the valleys, and as the sun rose a light wind was picking up off the water.

We began racing faster, and I leaned down over the bicycle with the building rush of speed. Looking ahead I saw the long line flattened against the side of the road, the riders low over the bicycles driving hard, and the small front group racing into the wind. As I watched the first break went clear and moved away down the road. Slowly there was the building excitement of the race. Maybe I would place at the finish. Maybe I would earn points. Maybe this year I would move up to the next category of racing. I swung into the wind, stood on the pedals, and sprinted up the line toward the front.

1

That was all in the spring. The winter before, in November, I began training for the new year. It was a cold gray morning. When I left my apartment I was wearing a jacket, shorts and leg warmers, and thick shoe covers, and I was still chilled. The clothes felt tight and uncomfortable after the break in the fall, and I went down the walk, out the gate, and swung my leg over the saddle. Searching for the pedals there was the solid snap as the cleats engaged and I pushed off into the street. For a moment the bicycle seemed unfamiliar, and then I sat down, the pedaling smoothed, and I rode away through the city of Berkeley.

I left the neighborhood near the college and came up through the residential area that climbed into the hills. The road was steep, and I slowed on the climb, stood on the pedals, and swung the handlebars back and forth, leaning my weight on each stroke. Slowly my body warmed, my breaths came faster, and I rounded above the first houses and looked back over the city and the bay.

Berkeley is placed on the east side of a wide bay formed by two peninsulas that encircle the water. Collectively the Bay Area forms an industrial metropolis, another Los Angeles or New York City, seven million people living together in a series of cities linked by freeways and highways. Now, in the winter, the bay was covered with mist, and the scene was almost unreal, with the sun shining over the mist, and only the points of the tallest buildings and the peaks of the mountains showing above the surface.

Along the east side of the bay there was a long ridge of hills. The hills formed a greenbelt of parks, and when you left the city on a bicycle you had to climb over the hills and through the parks to the country. When I came above the houses I could see the green of the parks, and I climbed away from the city and reached the ridge.

The road flattened and I sat down and shifted into a lighter gear. Through the trees was the open country with the heavy forest, the slopes covered with gray grass and chaparral, and the long backslope that spread down into the smooth rolling hills around the reservoir. I leaned forward over the bicycle and began riding faster; that is where all of the races will happen, I thought, out there on the roads in the country. That is where the season will unfold. I was filled with a distant forward-looking expectation for the races that were still far away, and I was happy to be riding again at the start of the year.

I began bicycle riding in New York City. My first bicycle, a blue machine made in France, was borrowed from a friend. Together we circled the streets and parking lots of the West Village in Manhattan, and when I got my own bicycle I began to explore more of the city, riding along the Hudson River to Battery Park, through Greenwich Village to Washington Square Park, and to the East Village. In the summer I rode in the country in Upstate New York, farmland and rolling hills covered in heavy green forest. I went on a bicycle trip through the Catskill mountains, rode to the Finger Lakes, and crossed the Adirondacks into Canada. Finally I got a racing bicycle, and began riding around the six-mile circuit in Central Park, and across the George Washington Bridge into New Jersey. Gradually I learned about the sport. I visited the old bicycle shops in the city, rode with the local teams, and followed the professional season in Europe. By the time I left New York I was training every day and racing on the weekends.

I had come to California for college where I was studying biology and English. Now, in my third year, twenty-two years old, I was considering options for the future: medical school, further study in biology or English, maybe a trip around the world. The best answer to the question of what I wanted to do after college was that I did not know. The only thing of which I was sure was that I wanted to race bicycles. It was the start of the season and I had begun training. I was preparing for the races, but I was also preparing to become a bicycle racer again, preparing to be subsumed by the world of sport, preparing to follow the one thing that I knew I loved for one year.

The road came out of the park and began the long descent into the country on the other side of the hills. I leaned down over the bicycle and shifted up through the gears with the building wind, and then I reached the first corner, sat up, and braked hard with the blast of air against my chest, let off the brakes, and rounded the corner, standing on the pedals bringing the gear back up to speed. The road went down through trees and came out below, and I flared my arms to slow the bicycle, and turned south along the hills.

On the other side of the hills it was cold and gray, and there were rows of cars passing toward the town of Orinda. Where we rode in the Bay Area there was no unbroken country, but rather towns separated by developments and protected land. We pieced together rides on the smaller roads where we could. Most of the rides came over the hills, down through the towns, and back up the canyons that climbed to the ridge. I followed the road through Orinda and the cars thinned. Then I reached the long gradual climb lined with bare trees and houses that led to Moraga.

When I came over the crest of the hill the mist was burning off and you could see the town below in the pale winter sun. The houses were showing through the trees, and behind were the forested hills leading back over the ridge. I coasted down the long descent, passing the new housing developments where there had been wild orchards, and came into the suburban town, with neat streets, ranch-style homes, shopping centers and parking lots. A smaller road led back into the country. I climbed a short hill, dropped steeply, and entered a forested canyon.

In the forest you were always blinded for a moment by the dark. It was cold and damp under the trees, and when you rode the other direction you broke out from the trees into the warm sun. Slowly my eyes adjusted, and then I could see the great firs and redwoods, tall and straight, with light filtering down from the tops, and heavy growth below. The road was wet and I climbed slowly on the steady grade. Then there were breaks in the trees, and I came out from the forest and rounded the first steep corner.

Looking back down the canyon you could see the town in the distance, and farther east Mount Diablo with the summit closed over in thin white clouds. Climbing in the sun it was hot, and I took off my gloves and opened the collar of my jacket. I shifted down through the gears, and slowly my breaths came faster, sweat began to rise on my skin, and there was the steady rhythm and deep building ache in my legs. It's always harder than you remember in the winter, I thought. You will grow stronger in the spring and summer, and what is difficult at the start of the season will be easy in the fall. The road turned and turned again, growing steeper near the ridge, and I stood on the pedals straining to turn the gear. Finally I reached the last steep pitch, pushed over the crest, and coasted on the flat road under the trees.

I was breathing hard and my heart was racing. Shifting into an easy gear I rode slowly along the ridge, my breaths falling, the feeling coming back into my legs. The sun was high and the mist had cleared off the bay. Below I could see the steep hills with the many expensive homes, the white flats of Berkeley, and across the water San Francisco,

Marin, and the coastal mountains outlined against the sky.

I thought of Anne. I wonder if she is still at the apartment. No, she has probably gone up to school to study. I met her two months before in the fall. It was a bright clear day and she was striding across the campus; her body was tall and slender, her shoulders back, her straight brown hair swept away from her face. She had tan skin and brown eyes, and when she laughed her face broke into a wide alive smile. She looked European or South American, but was really from the east coast, and had come to California as I had for college. She was studying English, and had one more year left before graduation. That summer we planned to live together.

I sat up on the bicycle and closed the collar of my jacket. There was a light wind off the bay and the trees were swaying overhead. The first ride of the season was over. It was a short ride, thirty miles, about two hours, but my body not yet accustomed to the effort and I was tired. I reached the descent and turned down toward the city.

2

Some days in the winter an inland wind held the mist over the water and it was sunny and bright. When I rode out to meet the others the wind was blowing, the sky was blue, and the city looked clean and white in the sun. Berkeley never felt like a real city coming from New York; there were only a few high buildings, over the houses you could see great towering palms, and there were overflowing gardens and yards along the streets. Close to the bay were warehouses and industry, on the flats residential neighborhoods, downtown the long ugly commercial strips of Shattuck and University Avenues, around the campus dormitories and Telegraph Avenue with all the shops and bars that catered to students, and finally the narrow winding streets in the hills. I lived near the college a few blocks below Telegraph Avenue, and I crossed the avenue and reached the cafe where we met for rides. Outside the cafe Dave, Chris, and John were waiting on their bicycles. They were wearing jackets and gloves, and they had extra clothing and full water bottles for the long ride. We rode south on the wide tree-lined streets, reached the winding road above the tunnel, and began to climb into the hills.

I met John, Chris, Dave, and Robert when I moved to California. I was riding along the ridge when they passed me in line, the four working together in smooth rotation, drafting close, racing down the descent. They were wearing matching jerseys, their faces were burned brown from the sun, and their bodies were lean and tan from riding. I followed them down the descent and caught them in the park, and we rode out into the hills. That summer they taught me about the rides and races in California. Climbing away from the city, listening to them talk and laugh, I thought how over the past years I had spent more time with them on the road than with my family, more time at the races than in college, more time training than working toward a career. And once again it was a cold winter morning and I was setting out for a long training ride.

John and Chris were riding on the front and Dave and I were following behind. Slowly my body warmed and I took off my gloves and opened the collar of my jacket. Beside me Dave rolled down his arm warmers, his tanned face flushed from the cold, his close-cropped blond hair dark with sweat, his legs working over the bicycle. Dave had the perfect form and easy natural grace on the bicycle that comes from many years of riding. Only a few years older than me, he had grown up in California, and he knew all the rides in the hills and surrounding country.

"How do you think it will be on the other side?" I asked.

"It's always wet along the ridge, and cold coming down the canyon."

As we climbed the houses fell away, we passed open grassy slopes and tall eucalyptus and pines, and we crested the ridge to the park. The road flattened, John and Chris swung off, and Dave and I came through on the front. In the cold wind I pushed harder and we rode through the patches of shade and bright sun under the trees. Below you could see the city of Oakland and the South Bay, and on the other side the park and dark green hills covered with mist.

When the road curved down toward Oakland we turned onto the descent that dropped into the canyon. The road was narrow and winding and fast and I let the others draw ahead, leaning down over the bicycle, the tires hissing on the wet roads, my eyes tearing from the cold. We raced through the forest, came out in the open, and began to climb once more. It was quiet with only the sound of the tires, the chains running through the gears, and our steady breaths. Gradually the road grew steeper. I dropped back and Chris pulled alongside.

"Come on," he said. "It's not a real climb." Chris was sitting up on the bicycle pedaling easily and breathing at a normal rate. How could he climb so well? There were no mountains in the Midwest. Chris had come to California from the Midwest for college, and we had started racing together in our first year. He was thin and light, with lean arms and legs and fine delicate features, and he rode well in the long road races with climbs. I was tall, over six feet and almost two-hundred pounds, and I was better suited to the flats and the short fast criteriums that finished with sprints.

I shifted down through the gears, and we came up through the park and over the crest of the climb. Below was the south reservoir with mist covering the water, green pines around the edge, and open protected land that extended to the developments. I sat up on the bicycle and drank, and we started the long descent into Castro Valley.

The descent was wide and smooth and fast, with banked sweeping turns, and you did not have to use the brakes. We rode in a line, drafting close, working in rotation, the first rider pulling into the wind and then dropping back as the next came through. I leaned over the bicycle with my head down, my back flat and low, and my legs spinning, and there was the dropping rush on the straights and the push of the corners and the gradual run as the country leveled and we came out along a wide open green. On the other side was Castro Valley. We rode through the empty gray city and turned onto a highway that lead toward San Ramon and the Diablo Valley.

There was heavy traffic on the highway and we hugged the line on the shoulder. The highway ran through the open country, past the ranches and housing developments, and came over the crest of the last hill. Below was the Diablo Valley. The valley stretched from the Upper Bay in the north, to the foothills around Livermore in the south, to the hills around Morgan Territory in the east. Below were the cities of San Ramon, Danville, and Walnut Creek, connected by freeways and suburbs, and covered now in the winter with a thick blanket of white mist. Rising above the mist was Mount Diablo. In the sun you could see the smooth tan foothills, the high brown mass of the peak, and the summit covered with light snow.

We started down into the valley and the mist closed around us like an enveloping cloud. John and I came through on the front, and we shifted gears and leaned forward over the bicycles in the cold. John rode with his shoulders hunched over the handlebars, his long legs turning awkwardly, and his thin pinched face staring ahead. Looking at him you would not have thought that he was an athlete, but John was one of the best bicycle racers that I knew. He had a spare, efficient form and a hard, driving intensity, and he rode well on the flats, on steep climbs, and even in criteriums when he made the breaks. He had graduated from college the year before, and he worked full-time in the city and raced on the weekends. We rode through Danville and reached the boulevard that led to Walnut Creek.

The boulevard ran past Mount Diablo in a long straight bordered by rows of bare trees. On the boulevard we all worked together silently, exchanging pace in smooth rotation, driving high gears, keeping the speed high. We wanted to cover that stretch of road as quickly as possible. The year before, on a similar cold gray morning, Dave, Chris, John, Robert, and I rode down the same boulevard. I came through on the front and dropped back on the inside, and then suddenly there was a great rush of air, a loud smacking sound, and a white blur in the road.

In a narrow tunnel of vision I saw bicycles, wheels, and water bottles flying through the air, and I braked hard and skidded to a stop. A white car was receding down the boulevard with the high sound of the engine fading. Dave was sitting on the grassy bank. Chris was climbing the far slope. John was standing behind. Far ahead I saw Robert lying in the road. I ran down the boulevard with my heart pounding and a cold feeling of fear in my chest.

Robert was lying with his arms folded in front of him and his knees drawn up to his chest and his head bent forward. When I saw him I knew that he was dead, but I leaned over and checked his wrist for a pulse, and then slid my hand under his jersey, feeling the cool moisture beaded on the outside, his skin warm and damp beneath. His heart was not beating, and I withdrew my hand and sat down beside him in the road. He looked like he was sleeping. His face was calm and his skin was flushed with a ruddy glow. From his mouth and nose and ears blood was flowing full and fast as from a faucet. The stream of blood ran over the road and formed a large bright red shining pool. The pool grew, steaming in the cold air, and then the flow gradually slowed, and the blood cooled and turned dark red and brown. The color had drained from Robert's face. His skin looked sallow and dull. He was dead.

My body was shivering and there was a ringing in my ears. My throat was constricted and my face was warm and wet. I realized that I was crying. Distantly I heard wailing sirens, and then there were police cars, ambulances with flashing lights, and television crews. A large crowd gathered and I stood up and walked away down the road. I was no longer crying, and I stopped and wiped my hands in the wet grass on the bank. In the distance I saw Dave, Chris, and John standing in a small group. Moments later I joined them. We had survived.

Among us Robert had been the strongest bicycle racer. He had just returned from college where he had studied Journalism and French, and he wanted to travel to Europe to write about professional bicycle racing. But that was over. The five of us had become four. Sometimes I rode down the boulevard without thinking about Robert and the accident, and other times I knew that my life, and the lives of the others, had changed that day on the road, and that we would never be the same again. Robert had been looking forward to the season. Just before the accident he and I had discussed his plans for the upcoming races. Maybe that is why we did not stop bicycle racing: We wanted to honor his memory. That winter we continued riding, and in the spring we started the first race of the season. We had not stopped now one year later.

As we rode down the valley the mist lifted, and we reached Walnut Creek and turned off the boulevard onto the smaller roads that led back toward Moraga. John and I pulled off the front and dropped back, and I sat up on the bicycle and coasted, feeling the tightness in my back and shoulders, the dull ache in my legs, and the numbed fatigue from the long ride. We had been on the road for more than sixty miles and four hours. I reached down and drank the last of my water, thinking of the miles that remained and the final climb of the day.

To distract myself I thought about the professionals in Europe. They were probably at the winter training camps. The first camps were usually held at the high ski resorts in the Alps or Dolomites where the teams began light training for the season. Then there were the camps along the Mediterranean where the weather was warmer and the teams began more serious training. Eventually there were press conferences and presentations, and you saw the first pictures of the teams on the road, the riders in pacelines, the directors driving in the team cars behind.

Bicycle racing was a wildly popular sport in Europe. There were many professional teams, large commercial sponsors, and important races through the year. In France, Italy, Belgium, and Spain bicycle racing was as popular as soccer all over the world, or baseball or football in the United States. Bicycling was part of their culture. Everybody rode bicycles, from the youngest children to the oldest grandparents. In Italy there was even a patron saint and chapel dedicated to bicycle racing: the Madonna del Ghisallo of the Ghisallo chapel in Lombardy.

Once I had visited the Ghisallo chapel. I lived in Italy for one summer bicycling with a small club in Veneto. The races were much faster than those in the United States, with large packs and many attacks, and you had to be strong enough to go with the attacks, stay with the breaks, and sprint when you came back into the towns for the finish. At the end of the summer I traveled across the country by train, and before I left Italy I rode to the Ghisallo chapel.

The chapel was a small building with a square stone bell tower, by the side of the road near the crest of a climb above Lake Como. On top of the bell tower there were rusted iron bicycle wheels and a cross, and above the arched entrance there was a frieze of the Madonna. When I reached the chapel I leaned my bicycle in the courtyard and walked beneath the archway into the building. When my eyes adjusted to the darkness I saw bicycles hanging from the ceiling and racing jerseys mounted in glass cases on the walls. There was a yellow jersey from Tour de France, a pink jersey from the Giro d'Italia, and a rainbow jersey from the world championships. There were also jerseys of famous Italian riders from Fausto Coppi to Gianni Bugno. One wall was covered with small plaques bearing the names of bicycle riders who had been killed on the road. There were hundreds of plaques of riders from around the World. Above the plaques a sign read: *Caddero Sulla Strada—Inseguendo un Sogno de Gloria—Che Raggiunsero—Nella Luce del Sacrificio—delle loro Giovani Esistenze.* They fell on the road—following a dream of glory—they reached the light in the sacrifice of their young existence.

Leaving the chapel I came out from the darkness into the bright sun in the courtyard. Below was Lake Como, shinning in the sun, with steep green slopes rising from the water, and the white walls and red roofs of towns on the slopes. The sky was clear and blue and there were small high clouds overhead. In the distance you could see the faint outline of the Dolomite mountains. Standing in the middle of the courtyard was a great bronze statue of two riders, one with his arm raised in victory, the other fallen to the road in defeat. On the stone base of the statue was an inscription: O, GOD, I BELIEVE IN THE BICYCLE, FOR WE HAVE MADE IT AN INSTRUMENT OF BOTH LABOR AND EXULTATION IN THE ARDUOUS JOURNEY OF LIFE. LET THIS HILL BE A MONUMENT TO OUR SPORT, WHICH IS ALWAYS BITTER IN VIRTUE AND SWEET IN SACRIFICE. The inscription and the sign in the chapel were filled with the kind of dramatic language that always made me uncomfortable, but standing in the courtyard of the chapel, the sun setting, looking out over the mountains, I thought of Robert, and I believed that I understood the words. It was only later that I understood their true meaning.

When we reached Moraga the mist had cleared and the wind had dropped. It was cold and the road was dry. Above the town you could see the bare hills and dark green forest leading back to the ridge. There was one more climb before home. We reached the canyon and began climbing toward the city.

3

When the rains came I was riding along the ridge. It was cold and gray and the bay was covered by heavy clouds. Slowly the clouds moved off the water, the sky grew dark, and the wind began to blow. Then it was raining and I sat up on the bicycle, pulled on my rain jacket, and closed the plastic collar. Maybe it's just a shower passing off the ocean, I thought. Sometimes the first rain did not last long, and afterward there were clear bright days like spring. The rain came harder, the tires began to hiss on the wet roads, and the spray soaked my legs and ran down my face with the taste of salt and dirt. I leaned down over the bicycle, shifted into a higher gear, and pushed harder to stay warm, looking out at the country gray and blurred through the rain.

The rains came in December and lasted for weeks, bringing snow to the mountains, filling the reservoirs, washing away the dead growth and gray grass in the hills, and covering the country with the light green spring grass. I remembered the summer showers in the East, the preceding days of thick heavy heat, the clouds coming over the country with the flashes of lightning beneath, the distant thunder, and the warm smooth rain over your arms and legs leaving you cool and refreshed after the showers passed. In Italy there were sudden storms in the mountains, with cold rain, sleet or snow, and you always carried a jacket even in the summer.

Gradually the rain thinned and the sky cleared. The wet country glistened in the sun. I was sweating beneath the plastic rain jacket, and I sat up on the bicycle and opened the collar, feeling the cool wind and the change in the air after the rain. Over the bay the clouds were massing heavy and dark, dragging curtains of rain behind, and I knew that it would rain again in the hills soon. I drank to wash the taste of dirt from my mouth, and turned down toward the city as the clouds moved off the water.

That night it rained long and steady and hard. It was the first real rain of the year, and Anne and I lay in bed, warm under the blankets, listening to the rain driving on the roof and the wind swaying the trees. Later the rain stopped and we dressed and went out into the city. The streets were quiet. Water was running in the gutters and the air was cool and clear. We walked past the college and reached the winding streets that led into the hills. Under the trees in the dark I stopped and held her and kissed her. I had only known her for three months but I thought that I loved her.

The next morning the sky was clear and the sun was shining. I climbed away from Berkeley with my jersey open and my arm warmers rolled down, feeling the sun and cool air on my skin. Below, the city was clean and bright, and the bay was clouded with run-off from the rains. I rounded above the houses and rode into the park, and there was the sudden fresh wet smell of the country, with leaves littered under the trees, rocks, and gravel strewn in the corners, and streams of water running along the road. The heavy grass over the slopes in the park was soaked through and matted down, and on the other side of the hills you could see the steel gray reservoir and bare white hills in the sun.

It would rain almost every day, with a few bright and sunny days, and days when the inland wind was blowing and it was dry and cold. Sometimes in the winter we drove down to southern California. We stayed in Los Angeles and rode in the canyons and hills to the north, and in the San Gabriel mountains that you saw through the haze across the basin in the morning. Or we drove down to San Diego, where it was even warmer, and rode in jerseys and shorts through the small towns on the palm-lined coast road, and into the mountains where you climbed above the foothills, through the national forests, and came out above the timberline with the view of the red-brown mountains of Mexico in the distance to the south.

That winter I did not travel to southern California or return home for the Christmas holiday. I wanted to stay in Berkeley with Anne, and I wanted to build the long steady base miles for the coming season. In January there was the Grand Prix d'Ouverture La Marseillaise. That was the traditional first race of the European professional season. Soon afterward we began racing in California. Then the year would revolve around the races.

I came out from the trees along the ridge. The sky had grown dark and the wind was blowing harder. I sat up on the bicycle and pulled on my jacket and gloves. The backslope spread down to the smooth rolling hills around the reservoir. I leaned down over the bicycle, shifted up through the gears, and began the long descent into the country.

4

I t was the first race of the year. We came over the headlands and down to the coast and the first break went clear. In the cool February air we raced along the water with bright sun and the wind blowing off the ocean. Soon the early break was caught, the pack slowed, and we came together into a large group.

When the chase was over I pulled to the side and dropped back down the line. It was late morning and the mist had burned away. Sitting up on the bicycle I drank, and then moved into the pack as we turned inland through the hills. The hills were dotted with oaks and covered with matted gray grass and a cover of close light green grass that came with the rains. It was spring and I was racing again, surrounded by the familiar mix of the pack on the road.

The race was eighty miles long and would take just over two and one-half hours to complete. It was always surprising to think of the distances you could covered in a race compared to a training ride. The speed was always a surprise. Only with racing did your body adapt to the speed: twenty-five miles per hour, thirty miles per hour at a steady pace. And I was only racing Category III. The Pro/I-II races were much longer and faster.

There were several categories of racing in the United States. There was Category V for beginners, Category IV for riders with some experience, Category III for intermediate riders, Category II for the best

local riders, Category I for the highest ranked amateurs who rode the
national championship and the Olympic trials, and finally the professional category.

Category II, Category I, and professional riders all raced together in
the Pro/I-II. Racing in the Pro/I-II was like playing in the minor
leagues; at the larger races you rode with professionals, and at the
smaller races you rode with the best in the country. I was satisfied to
have upgraded to Category III, but I always dreamed of upgrading to
Category II and racing with the professionals. I did not really believe
that it was possible, but each weekend I traveled to the races hoping to
place and earn points so that I could upgrade to Pro/I-II. This year I was
determined to do my best to upgrade to Category II.

In Europe the categories were different. Each country had its own
structure, and the professional category was much larger. They were
riding the Tour of the Med in France, or the Ruta del Sol or Tour of
Valencia in Spain. Maybe they were racing the Tour of Majorca, where
you could drop out of any stage and still start the next day. In the early
spring you saw the peloton all together for the first time; the riders
wearing new jerseys, arm warmers, and gloves, their legs bare in the
cold air and bright sun. The country in the South always reminded me
of California: smooth brown rolling hills and bare fields, light green
grass and pink just-flowering trees, roads along the coasts and mountains in the distance covered with snow.

After the races in the south the professionals traveled north for the
Fayt-le-Franc, Haut Var, Kuurne-Brussels-Kuurne, and Het Volk.
What did Het Volk mean? The people. They loved bicycle racing in
Brittany, Nord, Flanders and Walloon. The country was very different,
with low hills and woods, flat bare fields, short steep cobbled climbs,
and cold gray weather. The peloton raced on narrow, winding roads
through the fallow farmland and small industrial towns.

We came down from the hills and back to the water and the pack began racing faster. In the group there was the steady driving pace and gradual rising ache in my legs. How much longer is there, I wondered. We had passed the half-way point long ago, and I knew that there were at least twenty miles left before the finish. I had to hide from the wind and save my energy. You cannot get dropped, I thought. That is your first goal; you have to finish with the pack. Then, if you're feeling strong, you can try for the sprint. I stood on the pedals to stretch my legs and moved into the close-sheltered draft in the middle of the pack.

We turned away from the coast and began heading inland toward the finish. The road ran straight through the fields and the pack stretched into a long line. I leaned down over the bicycle, shifted up through the gears, and narrowed my body in the draft, with the drawn-forward, wind-rushing feeling of speed. Looking ahead I could see the line flattened against the side of the road and the small group on the front driving hard. In the distance was the finish and the banner over the road, and behind the light green brushed hills rising toward the mountains.

I knew that I would not make it to the front for the sprint; they were racing too fast and I was far behind. We came down the road onto the straight and the first riders moved right leading out the sprint. Then another line passed on the left driving up the gutter, and they were all sprinting with their heads down and the bicycles going from side to side. The front fanned out across the road, the banner drew closer, and there was the final surge over the line.

We swept under the banner and I sat up and coasted with the sudden draining release and happiness to have finished. The first race of the season is over, I thought. You did not get dropped and you came in with the pack. You just did not have the legs for the sprint. Riders were passing on both sides and stopping and turning around in the road. I shifted into an easy gear and let my legs fall on the pedals. Gradually my breathing slowed and the feeling came back into my legs. As I recovered there was already a voice in the back of my mind telling me that I should have done better at the finish. If I wanted to upgrade I would have to place in the races. Don't worry, I told myself. It's only the first race of the season. There will be many more races.

5

Two weeks after the first race of the season I rode into the hills on a bright sunny morning. The sky was clear and below you could see the white city and the bay swept flat by the wind. As I climbed my body warmed and the tightness in my legs disappeared. Slowly the city fell away below and I reached the ridge and rode into the park.

In the country the trees were full and green and the slopes were covered with heavy growth. On the other side of the ridge you could see the smooth green watershed around the reservoir. The country in the spring was extraordinary: the soft rounded sensual forms of the hills, the new close light green grass, the blossoming pink and white cherry trees, the many colored flowers, the fresh smell of the ground, and the warm breeze. All of the country would brown and burn in the summer, but now, in the spring, it was green and beautiful.

The spring semester had begun. Days in Berkeley were filled with classes, study sessions, exams, and conversations with my parents on the phone (Mother: Do you think you're riding your bicycle too much? Father: When are you going to stop riding that damn bicycle?). These were normal activities for any college student, however, my principal identity was that of a bicycle racer. It was almost as if I lived two separate lives: the everyday life of a young man working toward a career, and the regimented single-focused life of an athlete; asleep by eleven and awake by seven, no parties or late nights, Friday and

Saturday home early before the races. In the morning I noted my resting pulse and how my body felt from training, and in the afternoon I rode into the hills on my bicycle. I thought about rest and recovery, kept a diary of my progression, and planned the weeks and months of the season. Most of all I dreamed of the races.

In Europe the short early-season stage races were over. The Italian champion Gianni Bugno had won the Tour of the Med, taking the Mount Faron stage and the overall. Mount Faron was a beautiful stage. Cameramen always showed the peloton racing up the climb with the pines and white rocks and pale bright sun. Soon they would start Paris-Nice, the first stage race of the year, a week of racing that began in Paris and lead through the Massif Central to the Mediterranean. They pushed the snow to the side of the passes in the mountains, and the peloton rode between high white walls on wet black roads and came down to the Côte d'Azur. They called it "the race through the snow to the sun." In Italy there was Tirreno-Adriatico, which traversed the country from coast to coast. They called it, "the race between the two seas."

After Paris-Nice and Tirreno-Adriatico were the spring Classics: Milan-San Remo, the Tour of Flanders, Ghent-Wevelgem, Paris-Roubaix, Flèche-Wallone and Liège-Bastogne-Liège. There were many other races in those months: Critérium International, Flèche-Brabançonne, the Three Days of de Panne, the Semana Catalana, the Pays du Basque, the Tour of Aragon, the GP Cholet, the GP Rennes, and the GP Denain, but they were not as great as the Classics that came every weekend or every other weekend, starting in March and continuing all the way through April. When the Classics started the season truly began. Afterward the races passed quickly. Soon they would start Milan-San Remo, and then it would be July and they would be racing the Tour de France.

I came out from the trees along the ridge. It was warmer on the other side of the ridge and the grass was moving in sweeps over the hills. The road led down and disappeared beneath the trees. I sat up on the bicycle, opened my jersey, and went down around the corners into the country.

6

The first spring race weekend there was a road race in the Sierra foothills on Saturday and a criterium in the Great Central Valley on Sunday. We drove out from the city in the morning, came through the hills around Livermore, and climbed the long grade over the pass. On the other side of the grade was the Great Central Valley, a vast expanse that stretched from the Cascades in Northern California, to the Mojave desert in the south, to the Sierra Nevada in the east. Once it was a grassy savanna, but now it was covered fields and orchards and large farms, which yielded as much produce as most countries. We dropped into the valley and began the long flat run across the plain as the sun rose over the mountains on the horizon. Soon we reached the orchards and vineyards to the east where the land began to rise. Then we entered the foothills, rolling and green, with small hills and valleys and open spaces covered with thrusting gray rocks. Above were darker slopes of aspen and pine and finally the high snow-covered line of the Sierra.

When we arrived the sun was high and the sky was clear. Behind you could see across the valley, and far away the low hills near the coast covered with dark clouds. The others had just returned from Los Angeles and they were tan and fit from training. We changed into our jerseys and shorts at the car and rode down the hill toward the start.

I remembered how in Italy even the smallest races were organized around a town: You registered in crowded smoky bars, changed into your race clothing in bathrooms, pinned on your race number while standing on the sidewalk, and rode to the starts in the town squares. In California the road races were always far away in the country, and it was only for the criteriums that we came into the towns. We found the registration tables by the side of the road, and I picked up my number, checked that I had both water bottles and my rain jacket, and rode to the line.

The pack was staging under the banner and there were groups of riders gathered in the road and motorcycles and follow cars lined up behind. I rode up to the back of the pack and stopped over the bicycle waiting for the start.

When the pack formed the head official read the directions: the race was eighty miles long, there were four laps, the feed zone was on the hill after the start, and there was neutral support from the follow cars. After the directions they cleared the course, the driver mounted the motorcycle, and the follow cars started their engines. When the whistle blew we rolled away from the line.

The race began with a promenade. The motorcycle led slowly and we moved off down a road through the hills. I settled into the middle of the pack, the bright colors of the jerseys flowing together against the green country. Across the valley you could see the dark clouds moving inland with faint lines of rain below. In the foothills it was still bright and warm, and I pushed my arm warmers down over my wrists, and rode up alongside John.

"Hello."

"Are you going to win today?"

"I'm going to try."

"Do you think it will rain?" John sat up, steadying himself with one hand on my shoulder, and looked back across the valley.

"The clouds might run out," he said, "but if it rains the race is going to break apart."

We came over the crest of a small hill and the motor pulled away with the sound of the engine fading. Slowly the front stretched into a line and I leaned down over the bicycle and shifted up through the gears. We came down into the valley and flattened against the side of the road, the fields blurred on the sides, the mountains standing immobile in the background.

As we raced the rain clouds slowly moved over the valley. Then the wind began to blow, the sky grew dark, and it was raining. I sat up on the bicycle, unrolled my plastic rain jacket, drew the jacket over my shoulders, and closed the collar tightly. The pack came back together into a large group with the close nervous feeling in the rain, the lack of brakes on the wet rims, and the sudden changes in speed. I cleared the brakes and leaned forward over the handlebars. The country was gray through the rain, and you could not see the mountains covered by clouds. At the front they began racing faster.

When we came through the finish on the last lap it was raining hard and the wind was blowing. The pack was stretched into a single line. I was crouched over the bicycle and my hands were numb and I could not feel the pedals. With the rain and wind the race was breaking apart; there were gaps in the line, some riders were moving forward, others were dropping back, and you could not tell who was ahead and who was behind. I pushed harder, staring at the rear wheel of the rider ahead through the heavy gray driving rain.

Gradually the rain cleared and the clouds began to move away. Then the sun was shining and you could see the wet country and mist rising from the fields. I was riding with a small group, the bicycles covered with dirt, our legs streaked with gray water, our faces pale and wet. Slowly the cold faded in the sun and I sat up on the bicycle and tore off my rain jacket. Then I stood on the pedals and went up through the group to the front.

Ahead the road was empty. The pack was not in sight, and I turned my head and looked back down the road. There was nobody behind. We must be one of the last groups, I thought. We were not the last because the follow cars had not yet come around. John had been at the front when the race began to break apart, but I did not know about the others. Maybe they were ahead or with a chasing group. It did not matter. We had almost reached the finish. I sat down and drank to wash the taste of the dirt from my mouth, and then dropped back and moved into the middle of the group.

As we came down the road a motor drew alongside and the official waved us over to the side of the road. We moved to edge of the fields and the motor pulled away. Four riders passed in a driving line, their heads down, backs flat and low, legs turning high gears. It was the break from the Pro/I-II race. They had attacked at the start and moved clear in the rain. There were two Saturn riders, one Montgomery Bell, and one Pro Velo. They swept past and receded down the long straight through the fields.

I ducked my head and looked back under my arm and saw the second motor leading the rest of the Pro/I-II pack. We moved farther over to the side and the motor passed. Then there was a smooth building whir and sudden rush as the pack came over, the riders massed together with the bright colors of the jerseys, their backs tightly bunched, all their legs turning beneath, and the long line trailed behind.

We spread back out on the road as the pack receded. The break had a gap of about thirty seconds. With the pack chasing hard it was not enough, and I knew the break would be caught before the finish. The clouds had lifted over the Sierra and you could see the line of mountains over the valley. The country was drying in the warm sun. Looking ahead I saw the banner in the distance. We came down the road in the small group toward the finish.

7

The following day we drove back to the Great Central Valley for the criterium. We climbed over the pass, dropped into the valley, and reached one of the small farming towns in the country. The town seemed deserted on Sunday morning, and we left convenience stores and gas stations near the highway, and drove through the quiet residential neighborhoods on wide tree-lined avenues. When we reached the course we found the streets blocked with barricades, a banner strung over the straight, and a large platform for the officials. Rock music was playing from the stand, and the park was crowded like a festival. The Category IV race was underway, and we parked, changed into our race clothing, registered, and rode up to the course to watch the finish.

It was the last lap of the criterium and the pack was coming around for the sprint. I pulled up at the barricades and looked down the long empty straight. The crowd was silent and then the corner marshal raised his flag and one rider swept around the final corner into view. The crowd cheered, and the rider sprinted down the straight, keeping close to the barricades out of the wind. Then the pack rounded the corner and spread out in a flat haze, raising a light cloud of dust, the first riders sprinting with the line stretched behind. The lone rider was closer, and you could see his head down and his body working and the bicycle swaying from side to side. The crowd was cheering louder and the announcer was shouting and he swept past close to the barricades.

He's still a long way out, I thought, knowing what it was like to come down the straight with the pack chasing behind, knowing, also, what it was like to round the last corner at the front of the pack and sprint down the straight, not caring so close to the finish who was behind. The pack approached, and there was the building collective whir and flash of color as they swept past, the front racing hard, the riders at the back already sitting up and coasting.

As soon as the pack passed I ducked under the barricades and rode onto the straight. I always liked to warm up on the course before the criteriums, with the crowd watching from the sides and the charged feeling after the last race. I rode down the straight, standing on the pedals swinging the handlebars back and forth to bring the high gear up to speed, and then I sat down, swung toward the outside, and banked into the first corner.

There were no races like criteriums in Europe. In Belgium there were kermesses, but they were really circuit races that started in the towns, went into the country, and returned to the towns for the finish. In Italy there were *notturnos,* but they were only night races that started in the brightly lit town squares and ran through the narrow backstreets in the dark on each lap. In France there were criteriums but only in August after the Tour. Real criteriums, with short flat courses of less that one mile and many turns and straights and sprints, were only found in the United States, and they were the races where I rode best.

When I came around the course the pack was staging under the banner and I rolled up to the back of the group and stopped over the bicycle. The music was loud, the riders were talking and laughing, and I saw John, Dave, and Chris at the front. The day before John had taken the road race in a sprint from the front group. He had won his race. It was a great start to the season, and I knew that he would upgrade soon. Now, in the criterium, I wanted to do well, and I could feel the high nervous tension in my body. Finally the music stopped, the riders grew silent, and the head official walked into the road to read the race directions.

There were fifty laps, they would show the lap cards with ten to go, free laps stopped at five, and the pit was located before the line. The directions were always the same, and I only listened for the distance, lap cards, and free lap limit. The free lap limit meant that with five laps to go they no longer threw you back into the race if you had a mechanical or crashed, and when you went under the five there was always a change in the pack and the sudden fear and possibility of not making the finish.

The head official walked to the side and raised the starting pistol, the music began to play. I slid back in the saddle and leaned forward over the bicycle looking down the wide empty straight, with the barricades on the outside and the crowd behind the barricades and first corner bright in the sun. Then there was the sharp report of the pistol, the crowd cheered, and we rolled forward starting the race.

In criteriums there was no promenade and you began racing right away. I looked down, calming myself inwardly as I clipped into the pedals, and then I was sprinting down the straight with the others, surrounded by the pack, the sides blurring, my heart beating fast. We raced toward the first corner, swung to the outside, and braked hard. I leaned down and banked into the corner. When I came upright the riders at the front were already sprinting and the pack was stretched out single file. I stood on the pedals and sprinted up the line.

Criteriums. Lap after lap. The never ending rhythm: sprint, brake, bank into a corner, stand on the pedals, sit down, shift gears, tuck over the handlebars, make yourself smaller in the wind, stay on the wheel ahead, drive the pedals, sprint, sprint, sprint. One hour of intense exertion measured by the length of city blocks, and broken by the dangerous sweep of the corners. You stole small moments of rest when you could, drinking quickly, shaking out your legs, and then the speed would climb again, and you would dive into the next corner fighting the urge to brake, the pack tight and close, riders shouting, the front driving hard. Sometimes criteriums finished in breakaways, but mostly they finished in great bunched sprints. I loved them.

Late in the race we came past the finish with the crowd cheering and the music playing and the announcer shouting. The pack was driving hard and I looked to the side and saw the lap cards showing ten to go. You have to move up now, I told myself. You have to get to the front for the sprint. We came down the straight and rounded the first corner, and Dave rode alongside and motioned for me to take his wheel.

"Come on," he said, "let's go."

I dropped into the draft behind Dave and we went up the line and drew even with the front. On the backstretch the line swung over the road and we moved into the rotation. Dave came through and dropped back on the left, and I came through on the right. Then, on the other side of the road, a rider attacked and sprinted up the gutter with four others chasing behind. Dave jumped to the outside and bridged to the five, and I sat up and slowed on the front.

For a moment the pack did not chase, and then they massed forward on both sides and I dropped back and found a wheel. We stretched into a long line and I leaned down over the bicycle and drew myself forward on the saddle with the desperate spun-out wind-rushing feeling of speed.

The pack banked into a corner and came upright and I saw the break ahead on the straight. They were not yet far away. You can't bridge alone, I thought. Where is John? He's probably tired from yesterday. Maybe the others will catch them. No, I thought, I hope they stay away to the finish. Dave was in the right place when the attack went and he was strong enough to bridge. He deserved to place. I reached down and drank, and then replaced the bottle and looked back up the road. He was lucky, I thought. There was no way you could know they would go on the left. We came down the straight and rounded the final corner.

The pack was chasing hard, but the break slowly moved clear. They were working together in steady rotation, sweeping through the corners, sharing the pace in the wind. First they drew farther ahead on the straights, growing smaller in the distance, and then they were turning the corners before we came onto the straights, and we could no longer see them.

When the break disappeared the riders at the front slowed and the pack came back together into a large group. I sat up from the drops and shifted into an easy gear. Your race is over, I thought. You should have been at the front. You were at the front, I told myself, you were just on the wrong side of the road. At least Dave will place. He had a good sprint from a small group and there was a chance he could win. The break had reached the other side of the course, and from the backstretch you could hear the cheers of the crowd as they passed the line.

We came through the finish and I heard the bell ringing for the last lap. Usually when I heard the ringing bell there was the sudden rush through my body and the building excitement for the sprint, but the break had gone and there was no such feeling. There were six places in each race and six riders in the break. That was why they were working so well together, I thought, they knew they would all get points. There was no reason to sprint for seventh place. It was as good as last.

We rounded the first corner onto the backstretch and I drifted to the rear of the pack. Along the straight you could see the Pro/I-II riders sitting over their bicycles on the other side of the barricades. Across the park you could hear the cheers of the crowd as the break approached the line. We rode down the straight and came back around the course for the finish.

8

When I crested the headlands the green walls of the valley opened toward the coast and the ocean. The road led down along the side of the hills toward the blue water that was shining in the sun. Sitting up on the bicycle I closed my jersey and began the long descent, gaining speed on the straights, banking through the curves, braking around the steep corners, with the wind building and the smell of the ocean growing stronger. Finally the road ran out in the valley and I crossed the flat brown fields, reached the coast, and turned south along the water.

It was a bright clear spring weekend and you could see all the way down the long curve of the coast with the massed brown headlands, green sweeps of land, and yellow beaches. The beaches were shaped by the winter storms and scattered with driftwood, and farther out there were great black rocks pounded by heavy waves. On the other side of the road canyons spread back into the rolling green hills, leading up toward the high forested ridge of the Santa Cruz mountains.

It was spring break. Instead of traveling south for vacation like most of my classmates I stayed in California to train. In Europe they were racing the spring Classics. The first Classic of the season was Milan-San Remo or La Primavera. The riders started in front of the cathedral in the Piazza Duomo in Milan, crossed the Lombardy plain and the Apennines, climbed the Turchino pass with the snow pushed to the side

of the road, broke out of the tunnel to the Mediterranean, and came
down past the white cliffs to the coast, where they raced through the
towns and over the Capo Mele, Capo Berta, Cipressa and Poggio,
before the finish in San Remo. The Frenchman Laurent Jalabert had
attacked on the Poggio and come into San Remo with one other rider
to take the sprint on the Via Roma. Early in the season he had won the
Arenal stage at the Tour of Majorca, the Benidorm stage at the Tour of
Valencia, and the overall at Paris-Nice and Critérium International. He
was the first real French champion since Laurent Fignon in the eighties.

Two weeks after Milan-San Remo there was the Tour of Flanders.
The riders began in Bruges, raced through the flat open country and
many small brick and slate towns to the North Sea, and came back over
the climbs to the finish in Meerbeeke. The old cobbled climbs were
famous. The Kwaremont had been taken out of the race because the
road was so narrow that the follow cars could not pass, but there were
still the Mur de Gramont, the Bosberg, and the Koppenberg, which
was so steep that only the very first riders made it over the summit, and
the rest had to get off their bicycles and walk. The Belgian Johan
Museeuw had broken away on the Mur de Geraardsbergen and come
over the Bosberg and into Meerbeeke alone to take Flanders for the
second time in three years. It was usually a Belgian who won, and
Museeuw was the best Classics rider of his generation.

After Flanders there was Ghent-Wevelgem, flat and windy, with
the famous climb of the Kemmelberg before the finish, then Paris-
Roubaix, very long and flat running over the old cobbled roads of
northern France, and finally the Classics in the Belgian Ardennes;
Flèche-Wallone, the Walloon Arrow, a winding race with the many
climbs of the Mur de Huy, and Liège-Bastogne-Liège, called La Doy-
enne, long and hard, with the long steep climbs of the Stockeu, the
Haute Levee, La Redoubte and the Côte des Forges. Liège-Bastogne-

Liège was the last spring Classic.

The spring classics were special. They were the races that you always imagined in your mind. You saw yourself racing along the coast in Milan-San Remo, crossing a barren field on a cobbled road in France, climbing a steep hill through an old town in Belgium. There were other races afterwards: Amstel Gold, Paris-Camembert, the Settimana Bergamasca, but there was nothing of real importance until the stage races in May.

Along the coast I reached the headlands and began the first long climb. Gradually the road grew steeper and I slowed and shifted down through the gears, my breaths coming faster, the ache building in my legs, the heat rising in the sun. As I climbed the headlands fell away, the wind dropped, and it was quiet, with only the steady sound of my breaths and the light breeze moving over the hills.

A car approached from behind and I moved to the shoulder. The car drew alongside and slowed and I looked up from the road.

"Anne!"

"Hello."

"How did you know I was here?"

"You said you were riding down the coast and I thought I would meet you."

I sat up on the bicycle and grasped the window frame with the car pulling me up the climb. Anne smiled and laughed, pulled a strand of hair away from her mouth, and laughed again. She was wearing a light shirt and bathing suit with a towel knotted around her waist, and the wind was blowing her hair around the car. Beside her on the seat was a water bottle, blanket, and change of clothes.

"Do you want to stop?"

"No. Let's drive farther on and find a beach."

Anne leaned across the seat steering with one hand and held out the bottle of water, and I took the bottle, drank, and crested the climb.

On the downhill I raced ahead of the car. I slid back on the saddle, placed my hands close together near the stem, and crouched over the bicycle in a low tuck. The road ran out on the flats and I let my momentum carry me until I slowed, and then sat up and began riding into the wind. Anne pulled ahead and I moved into the draft behind the car. In the draft the gear was light and I shifted into high gear and spun the pedals. I could hear the wind above and on the sides of the car, and looking ahead I could see Anne in the mirror concentrating on the road.

For a long time there was a split between school and bicycle racing, and I could not find a woman with whom I could share both sides of my life. In Italy I had met a woman named Maria. She was the cousin of one of the Italian riders in our club. Her father was from Sicily, and she had thick black hair, dark skin, and a strong proud face. When we went on bicycle rides she would drive ahead and meet us in the piazzas of the towns or at the tops of the mountain passes with picnic lunches, and at the races she would wait at the finish with bottles of water and tell us how we had placed. But that was in Italy. Now in California I had met Anne. There was no longer a split between the two sides of my life, and I was happy to be driving along the coast sharing the day.

To the south the road dropped into into the dunes, running almost below the level of the water, and I could just see over the tops of the rolling white sand to the flat blue ocean. Then the road curved above and came back into the hills, and there were slopes of high green grass moving in the wind, rows of tall swaying eucalyptus, and dark green pines and white cypress along the cliffs.

Anne drove ahead and pulled off the road and parked on the shoulder. When the car pulled away the wind that had been blocked came up with the loud roaring sound, the gear was heavy, and suddenly

I was tired from holding the pace. I came slowly down the road and coasted to a stop, and then she was in my arms, her body pressed against mine, her hair cold and silky from the wind, her arms around me as we kissed. She pulled away and pursed her lips, "You're salty!"

Behind the car I stripped off my jersey and shorts, wrapped the towel around my waist, and washed myself with the water from my bottle. My skin was burned from the sun and the water was cool. I smoothed away the rough salt and sweat, toweled dry, ran my fingers through my hair, and changed into the clothes Anne had brought. We locked the bicycle in the car, took the towel and blanket, and began walking down toward the coast.

A small brown dirt path led into a stand of pines. We came under the trees with the sharp smell of the needles and the soft broken orange light. Then through the branches we could see the blue sea shining in the sun. The path came out from the trees on a high cliff. Below was a small cove and beach. The waves were coming up in regular white lines and the wind was blowing in off the water.

We went down the path to the beach, took off our shoes, and walked barefoot over the sand to the cliffs, where we spread the blanket on the sand and lay down. Our bodies formed a hollow in the sand and the cliffs blocked the wind. Anne rolled over and rested her head on my chest.

"Can we stay like this?"

"It's perfect."

I put my arm around her shoulder and ran my hand through her long brown hair and kissed her smooth tan skin. Gradually her breaths slowed, her body became heavy in my arms, and she was asleep. I lay in the sand looking up at the high blue cloudless sky, listening to the wind swaying the trees and the waves on the shore. The fatigue from the ride faded and I closed my eyes and slept.

When I woke the sun had moved over the water. Anne was still sleeping with her head on my chest and her arms around my shoulders. I did not want to wake her and I shifted carefully so that my head lay on my outstretched arm looking down the long white curve of the beach. The waves were breaking on the rocks and far out the flat sheet of the ocean and the sky came together on the horizon. Away from the road, lying on the beach with Anne, it seemed that we were the only two people on the whole coast.

That afternoon we walked all the way down the beach and followed a hard graded dirt road back to the highway. We drove home over the mountains and returned to Berkeley before dark. It had been a long wonderful weekend.

9

The second week of April, on Easter Sunday, I rode in the morning, returned home, and walked up to the bar on Telegraph Avenue. It was bright and warm and the avenue was crowded with people. The bar was empty and I sat down at the counter and asked the bartender to turn on the television. It was the day of Paris-Roubaix.

The European races were only shown in the middle of the day or late at night when there were no other conventional sports to run. The coverage came from a European feed and the commentary was usually in English, though sometimes French or Italian. France was nine hours ahead and the race had already finished. The bartender switched through the channels, and suddenly on the screen I saw the riders gathered in the Place du General de Gaulle in Compeigne for the start of Paris-Roubaix.

The Place du General de Gaulle was bordered by old stone buildings and there were bare winter trees around the square and Belgian and French flags over the crowd. On one side was the stage with the announcing stand, and on the other was the high metal gantry with the name of the principal sponsor, La Redoubte, and the blue and white Fiat and television station placards. The square was crowded with reporters, team personnel, and race commisaires. The riders were circling on their bicycles or waiting at the team cars, and you could hear the music playing and the announcer calling the names one by one as the riders came onto the stage to sign-on and the crowd cheered.

It looked bright and sunny and cold. The people in the crowd were dressed in coats and scarves and the riders were wearing arm warmers and jackets. It was dry and I knew the course would be fast. The riders gathered under the gantry, the director conducted a short ceremony, and the peloton rolled forward with a great cheer from the crowd. The caravan swung in behind, and slowly they made their way out of the square into the streets of Compeigne.

Paris-Roubaix is almost one hundred years old, I remembered. They called it La Pascale because it was traditionally held on Easter Sunday, or La Reine de Classiques, the Queen of the Classics. They used to start in Paris and race straight down the main road to Roubaix, but now they started in Compeigne and the parcours led through the flat country of Aisne and Nord following the many short stretches of old cobbled road. There were twenty-two stretches of cobbled road in all, with the famous runs through the Arenberg forest, Ennevlin, and Carrefour de l'Arbre, and it was because of these roads that Paris-Roubaix was also called Le Enfer du Nord, the hell of the north.

The cobbled roads were slick and muddy when wet, broken and dusty when dry, and they did not even start until Troisvilles at one hundred miles. The whole race was one hundred and sixty miles long, and after seven hours of racing over the rough roads, across the pounding cobbles, the riders reached Roubaix and came into the smooth high velodrome for the finish. It was a beautiful race.

When they reached the outskirts of Compeigne the promenade ended and the great procession spread out on the road. At the front were the advance cars and gendarmes on motorbikes clearing the course. Then there were the commisaire cars, the red car of the director, and the peloton. Behind was the long line of team cars, each painted team colors with the many bicycles and wheels mounted on the roof, the even longer line of press cars, commisaire cars, and radio cars, and finally the motorcycles: commisaire motors, television motors with the cameramen standing on the footpegs and the tall cone-topped transmission poles, photography motors, sleek yellow service motors with the mechanics crouched on the back holding spare wheels, and small light off-road motors that followed the riders over the cobbled roads. The helicopter showed them from above and you could see the procession stretched for several miles, moving slowly through the country, with the shadow of the helicopter flowing over the fields.

In the middle of the procession the peloton looked very small. The front slowly stretched into line and the first rider sprinted away and moved clear on the road. The early breaks did not matter and I looked away from the television. The real race did not begin until they reached Troisvilles.

At the end of the counter the bartender shook his head.

"I don't understand," he said. "You can never tell what's going on."

It was hard to understand bicycle racing when you saw it on television. They would show the peloton from the helicopter, and then they would cut to the motors and suddenly you were close among the riders, moving and flowing and changing positions on the road. Sometimes the peloton was together in a large group, sometimes it was stretched into the long line, and sometimes they showed small groups or single riders. There were always different riders at the front, and these were almost never the riders who won, who seemed to come from behind and cross the line first.

I told the bartender to watch how when they were all together they were riding slowly, and when they were stretched in line they were racing faster. You could tell the speed also by looking at the country as they passed, the gears they were riding, or the expressions on their faces. The races are very long, I said, and no one rider can stay at the front in the wind for the whole distance. That's why they're always riding one behind the other and rotating at the front; they're sharing the work in the wind. Don't think of who's winning at any given moment. There are only a few riders who can win and they're the team leaders. The riders at the front for most of the race aren't the leaders but the team workers, called *domestiques* in French, whose job is to set the pace, make the breaks, chase other teams, and carry food and water and clothing between the peloton and the team cars. Sometimes domestiques win, but not often in a race like Paris-Roubaix, which is so difficult. Don't worry if you can't tell the leaders right away, I said. When the real racing begins the leaders will come to the front. Just watch the riders and their efforts and expressions, and look at the country, and slowly the story of the race will develop.

We sat together at the counter and watched the peloton ride through Aisne. The country was flat and green with gentle rises and sweeps of land, and over the plain you could see the green and yellow and brown fields, the rolling cover of woods, farmhouses dotting the country, and spires of churches in the distance. During the early running they did not show all of the race and only started the continuous coverage at Troisville. When they passed the half-way point at Saint-Quentin the early breaks had been caught and the peloton was all together.

It was wonderful to feel that you were traveling with them. Watching the professionals was always beautiful: the way they pedaled so smoothly on the high gears and moved through the peloton. When I thought of the distances they covered and the speeds they rode it was hard believe that I would ever race in the pro-am category. As I imagined their lives and careers, they seemed almost God-like. Were they stronger, or more courageous, or more determined than other people? No, I thought, they simply had more powerful hearts, greater blood vessels, finer capillaries, faster nerves, and developed muscle fibers. Then, in addition to their physical attributes, they had honed their skills through years of training, hours of hard work, and a mono-maniacal obsession with their sport. Maybe if you had grown up in Europe you would be one of them. That is what I told myself, but it was not easy to believe watching them in the bar.

As the race approached Troisville they began racing faster. The peloton stretched into the long line, and you could see the domestiques at the front and the team leaders moving forward. Finally they came into the town racing fast and flat out as if it were the finish. It was really only the beginning; they had reached the first stretch of cobbles, sector twenty-two. Now the sectors would come in quick succession, alternating with smooth paved roads, counting down all the way to Roubaix.

The Romans first built the cobbled roads. They were covered with small close-set stones or large square yellow granite blocks called *pavé*, worn down in parallel ridges by the wheels of the horse drawn wagons, carts, tractors, trucks, and cars, heaved up with protruding sections, and sunken into low holes hidden by standing water. There were many crashes on each sector, the race always broke apart on the pavé, and all the riders wanted to be at the front when they came out of Troisvilles.

They raced through the town, rode up a short hill along a field, and took the left hand turn onto the pavé. There was a large crowd standing in the field and when the riders turned onto the pavé a great cheer went up from the crowd. Immediately a cloud of dust lifted from the road and streamed backward, covering the peloton, swirling in the wind from the helicopter rotors, and within the light brown dust, illuminated by the dim yellow lights of the follow cars, you could see the long undulating line of riders. Then, just as quickly as they had turned onto the pavé, the riders came back onto the pavement in a rush and the cloud of dust blew away across the field.

Sector twenty-two of pavé was over. Twenty one sectors remained. The riders slowed, the peloton came together, and you could see the domestiques dropping back through the caravan to leave clothing at the team cars and pick up water for the leaders. It looked warmer and the sun was high and clear. They were approaching the next sector of pavé. Ahead was the banner with the green La Redoute, the number and name of the sector in black, and the distance covered and that which remained in red. They raced over the sectors at Quievy, Solesmes, Querenaing, Famars and Valenciennes, and then they passed the ironworks and the entrance to the old coal mine and came onto sector fifteen through the Arenberg forest.

The Arenburg was the most famous sector of pavé in Paris-Roubaix. There was almost always a selection in the forest, and all of the leaders were at the front when they came onto the long straight that fell in a gradual line between the two grassy banks, with the smooth brown dirt paths on the sides, the thick forest behind, and the bare trees that reached overhead to form a corridor. There was a great crowd standing on the grassy banks and along the dirt paths and in the road, kept back by the gendarmes in the black suits and white caps, and the people in the crowd were stamping their feet to stay warm, shielding their eyes with their hands, and looking down the road. Above you could see the blue sky and the helicopter hovering over the faint cloud of dust in the distance that was the peloton. Then the red lead car came into view, the headlights shining yellow through the dust, with Jean-Marie Leblanc, the director of the Société du Tour de France, standing out of the roof waving the crowd back. The trees trapped the rising dust, the sound of the cars and motors, the horns and high-low high-low sirens, the heavy beating of the helicopter, and the steady cheers of the crowd that pushed into the road and closed over the pavé, parting only at the last moment as the peloton passed, and the riders came straight down the center of the pavé or on the smooth dirt paths on the banks, switching sides and pushing the crowd out of the way to avoid the worst sections. From a distance they seemed smooth and fluid moving over the pavé, but when they showed them from the motors you could see the bicycles vibrating and bouncing, their flesh shaking, their muscles tensed, and their faces set with their cheeks drawn back and their eyes squinted in the dust looking down the road.

When they came out of the Arenberg the first selection had been made. The peloton was much smaller with only one hundred riders left. Some had dropped back to pace their leaders to the front, some had been caught behind in crashes on the pavé, and some had stopped racing because their work was done for the day. Most had been left behind because the speed was simply too fast, and many would abandon at the first feed zone where the team cars were waiting. A few would continue along the road, far behind the peloton, to say that they had finished Paris-Roubaix. At the front of the peloton you saw the leaders: Sean Yates, Gilbert Duclos-Lassalle, Franco Ballerini, Gianluca Bortolami, Andrea Tafi, Museeuw, Andreï Tchmil. They were all strong powerful riders who could push the high gears over the pavé. Vlaeminck, the King of Paris-Roubaix, had won four times. They said you had to be lucky to win, but because the same riders went well every year you knew there was skill to riding the pavé; most of all they said that you had to love the race.

Yates rode Paris-Roubaix more than ten times, I remembered. He was one of the riders who crossed the English Channel to race on the continent; first Tom Simpson, then Jones, Herety, Sherwin, and Yates, from Scotland Dave Millar, and from Ireland Early and Kimmage, and the champions Sean Kelly and Stephen Roche. Together they called them the Foreign Legion. Now Yates raced for the Motorola team from the Unites States.

The Frenchman Duclos-Lassalle, thirty-eight, was the oldest rider in the peloton. He had raced with all the great champions of the last two decades—Eddy Merckx, Bernard Hinault, Greg LeMond—and he had always been a domestique. Then he won Paris-Roubaix with a beautiful solitary breakaway. The following year he went with an attack by a young and very strong rider named Franco Ballerini, and when they came onto the velodrome in Roubaix Duclos-Lassalle won the sprint. Now he was a champion and the leader of the French Gan team. The week before he had taken a stage of the Pays du Basque.

Franco Ballerini rode for the Italian Mapei-GB team with Gianluca Bortolami, Andrea Tafi, and the Belgian Johan Museeuw. Then there was Andreï Tchmil with the Belgian Lotto team. Tchmil was one of the Red Guard, a group of riders from the former Soviet Union who had turned professional with Alfa Lum when the USSR collapsed. You never knew their history, and you heard about the closed sports institutes with the almost-religious secrecy, and most of the riders were very good when they turned professional. The year before in Paris-Roubaix it rained and the pavé was covered with thick black mud. Tchmil broke away alone and when he came onto the velodrome in Roubaix his face and jersey were black with the mud and you could not tell what team he rode for as he slowly circled the high white track. He was the first Russian to win Paris-Roubaix. In the spring he had placed third at Het Volk and third again at Flanders.

On the smooth paved roads Tafi came to the front and attacked. He sprinted down the road, let the bicycle come forward beneath him, and settled into the steady pace, his back flat and low, his legs turning the high gear, his long thin tan face looking ahead. At the bottom of the television screen the small window came up with his number, 27, name, A. Tafi, team, Mapei-GB, country, Italy, and the words *tête de la course*, head of the course. The French always had the best terms for cycling: the breakaways were *echappes*, escapes, and the chasing groups were the *poursuivants*, pursuers. In Italian there was the *gruppo della testa*, the group at the head, the *fugitivi*, the fugitives, and the *gruppo insegui-torie*, the chasing group.

One rider bridged to Tafi, then another, then another, and finally the peloton caught the break and they all slowed and came back together. One rider counter-attacked, Tafi bridged, two more came across, and the four moved clear of the peloton.

In the break were Tafi, Dietz, a German with Deutsche Telekom, Viatcheslav Ekimov, and Eric Vanderaerden. Echimov was another of the Red Guard. When he was young he had set world records on the track and won a stage of the 1991 Tour de France, and now he rode for the Dutch Novell team. Vanderaerden was also a champion. I remembered watching him in 1985 when he won Flanders in the rain and in 1987 when he won Paris-Roubaix. Now, eight years later, he had not lived up to the expectations of his country and had been sacked by the Belgian teams, and was riding for the small Italian Brecialat team. He looked much older but he was again racing at the front in Paris-Roubaix.

They showed them from the side and you could see Tafi leading the break in the blue Mapei-GB jersey, Dietz in the white and pink Deutsche Telekom, Echimov in the red and white Novell, and Vanderaerden in the blue and yellow Brecialat. Behind was the peloton with the bright massed colors of all the teams. There were twenty teams in the race: Mapei was an Italian construction company; Deutsche Telekom, a German telecommunications company; Novell, a Dutch software company; Brecialat, an Italian dairy distributor; Motorola, an electronics company; Gan, a French clothing manufacturer. The riders were really advertisements, and the names of the principal sponsors and secondary sponsors covered the jerseys, shorts, socks, gloves, helmets, and team cars. The large professional teams cost several million dollars and the investment was returned when the teams showed in the newspapers and on the television and the road.

It was the working class people around the country who watched bicycle racing. At the turn of the century and after World War I, the impoverished people of Europe identified with the riders racing on rough roads, over the mountains, through the broken country in all weather, and the sport became popular. That was still the background of most riders, and you always heard the stories about the champions who would have been farmers or factory workers or bricklayers if they had not started racing. When Paris-Roubaix passed all of the people from the surrounding country came to watch the race; along the roads you saw farmers with muddy rubber boots and black berets, women wearing handkerchiefs, old women wrapped in black shawls, old men in suits, mothers holding babies, packs of young boys, fan clubs with the great banners and flags. In the towns all the shops and businesses were closed, and there were crowds of workers and groups of schoolchildren in uniform in the streets, and nuns and priests in front of the churches. Many people also traveled to see Paris-Roubaix; in the fields and ditches along the road there were rows of car and bicycles, and when the race passed the spectators set off in a rally to catch the riders again farther along the course.

They showed the peloton from above and the team cars came up along the right with their lights flashing and horns honking and wheels half in the ditch, reached the front, swerved back into the road, and accelerated up to the break. That means the time gap has gone over one minute, I thought. They switched to the first motor and the gap came up on the screen at 1:12. Tafi dropped back to the Mapei-GB car and you could see him talking to the director Juan Fernandez through the open window, with the manager Patrick Lefèvre in the passenger seat and the mechanic behind. Fernandez gestured and shouted over the sound of the wind, holding a water bottle in his hand with Tafi holding the bottle also, pulled along by the car, and then Fernandez accelerated, still holding the bottle, and released the bottle, slinging Tafi forward. Tafi took the bottle cleanly, leaned down over the bicycle, and went back up the road to the break. He sat on the last wheel and did not pull through the rotation. Fernandez must have told him not to work, I thought. Mapei-GB started the break, they had many strong riders behind, and they would make the other teams chase.

The race was moving through Nord toward Belgium and you could see the flat green and brown fields on the sides, the light tan roads, the rolling green hills, the woods and farmhouses, and the tall Flemish windmills with square stone bases and broad rectangular vanes. They passed through Somain and Tilloy and came off sector twelve on the outskirts of Orchies, and then they were racing through the town with the rows of houses, cheering crowds, waving flags, and ringing church bells. The gap came up at 2:47 and they reached the motorway and turned onto sector eleven.

When the peloton reached sector eleven the front rounded the corner and bunched and slowed, riders fell into the middle of the road, and the word *chute*, crash, came up at the bottom of the screen. The riders spread out and streamed past the crash and the whole caravan stopped behind. Then the mechanics were out of the cars running with the spare wheels in their hands, and the riders were back on their bicycles sprinting down the road, and the caravan began moving again. There was one rider left standing on the outside of the corner. It was Andreï Tchmil. The crowds closed over him and he waited calmly holding his wheel overhead to signal the Lotto car. He looked shorter that he did on a bicycle, with muscular legs, a wide tan Slavic face, and close cropped brown hair covered with sweat and dust. The cars were passing and small groups of riders working their way up through the caravan, and then the Lotto car swerved to a stop, the mechanic ran from the car and quickly changed the wheel, holding the bicycle upright between his knees, and Tchmil was back on the bicycle, standing on the pedals to bring the gear over, with the mechanic running alongside pushing him up to speed. It was always exciting to watch the wheel changes. Usually they took less than thirty seconds and the riders were quickly back in the race. The mechanic gave a final lunging throw, and Tchmil sprinted away down the road.

After Orchies the peloton began to chase. Yates, Duclos-Lassalle, Bortolami, Ballerini, Museeuw, and Tchmil who bridged after the crash all came to the front, and slowly the time gap began to fall. At Merignies it was 2:15. At Bersee 1:30. At Attiches 1:15. When the gap went under one minute they pulled the follow cars and riders began to attack. One rider would sprint down the road and the peloton would stretch into the long line, slow, and come back together into the large group; then another rider would attack and again the peloton would stretch into the long line, slow, and come back together into the large group. With the constant changes in speed the sixty riders broke apart into small groups of ten and fifteen and thirty, or three and eighteen and twenty, or one and fifteen and twelve, and gradually, each time the peloton came back together, there were fewer riders at the front.

As they reached the town of Seclin one rider broke away. They showed him racing through the streets and I saw the pink jersey and blue shorts but could not tell the team or rider. The motor picked him up on the road and I saw that it was Johan Capiot, the Belgian national champion in 1994, who had won the Fayt-le-Franc in March. In 1992 he was third in Paris-Roubaix, in 1994 he was sixth, and now he was riding for one of the smaller division two Italian teams, Refin-Catina Tollo. Bortolami was chasing behind, he bridged after Seclin, and the two began working together on the road.

Now Mapei-GB had Tafi in the break, Bortolami behind, and Ballerini and Museeuw in the peloton. It was like a chess game; they kept attacking, advancing their position, and forcing the others to work. I did not know who was leader. Sometimes on a team like Mapei-GB there was no one leader and they let the strongest rider show on the road. Museeuw is probably the leader, I thought. He won Flanders the week before and he was leading the World Cup, but he had crashed at Ghent-Wevelgem on Wednesday and injured his knee. Maybe Ballerini is the leader. He placed second at Paris-Roubaix and won Het Volk in February, but he also crashed at Ghent-Wevelgem and injured his shoulder. Bortolami won the World Cup the year before, but he had not shown in the spring. That leaves Tafi, I thought. He was a domestique and had worked for others for many years and I would have loved to see him win, but he could not be the leader. It was a business, and while you loved to see certain riders win and wished they could all have a chance, you knew that was not possible.

The peloton was racing toward sector seven. The front was stretched in line along a field, and then, on the outside, moving toward the front, you could see one rider with his jersey obscured. The rider gradually gained speed, standing on the pedals and swinging the bicycle back and forth, and then he reached the front, jumped on the pedals, and attacked into the open. It was Ballerini.

He sprinted away with his head down and the bicycle going from side to side, and then sat down and shifted gears and looked back over his shoulder. He had gotten the gap, and he leaned forward and settled into the high steady pace. They showed him from the side with the green field and low treeline behind, and then they switched to the helicopter and the camera panned upward and the country spread out with the green and brown fields, the cover of woods, the long straight gray road, the light tan pavé, and the one rider growing smaller on the road.

The motor picked up Capiot and Bortolami. They were working together, and Bortolami came through on the front and looked back over his shoulder. When he saw Ballerini coming up he slowed, dropped back, and brought Ballerini across. Capiot did not turn around; he held the pace, and when Bortolami and Ballerini bridged they went straight to the front, and Capiot swung in behind.

Now it's clear, I thought. Ballerini is the leader of Mapei-GB and the others are working for him. It was wonderful to watch the race change on the road; first there was the break, Capiot attacked and Bortolami bridged, the two worked together until Ballerini attacked, and then Bortolami dropped back and brought up his leader, and now the two Mapei-GBs were riding at the front and Capiot was following behind.

They came onto sector seven and Capiot began to fall back. There was no longer the smooth driving flow over the pavé, and you could see his arms tensing and his legs straining to push the gear. Ballerini and Bortolami pulled away, the gap opened, the wind came up, and Capiot lost a bicycle length. Just hold on, I thought. Just hold on to the road and you can recover. Capiot stood on the pedals and sprinted to close the gap, drawing onto the last wheel and leaning down over the bicycle out of the wind, and then the wheel pulled away again, the gap opened, the wind came up, and he lost two bicycle lengths. They turned a corner on the pavé and Capiot cut to the inside, overcorrected, swerved onto the grassy bank with his wheels sinking into the ground, and came back onto the pavé slowed almost to stop. The crowd cheered and Capiot raised himself from the saddle and stood on the pedals leaning all his weight on each stroke, riding slowly with his bicycle bouncing and shaking and his arms slack and his head hanging down. There is no way he will catch them now, I thought. Bortolami and Ballerini receded straight down the crowned center ridge of the pavé, and the motor picked them up on the smooth roads outside Templemars. They were working hard, sweeping through the corners, driving down the straights, closing on the break.

Dietz, Echimov, and Vanderaerden were leading the break. If Bortolami and Ballerini bridge there will be three Mapei-GB riders at the front, I thought, and they still have Museeuw in the peloton. They came through a town past low white houses and reached the motorway, and Tafi attacked. He sprinted down the left side of the road, let the bicycle come forward beneath him, and settled into the long low position over the bicycle.

Tafi has finally attacked, I thought. After all the years of working as a domestique he attacked in Paris-Roubaix. I guess he did not know the others were chasing. They pulled the team cars long ago, and there was no way to get the time checks. Or maybe he knew. Maybe he knew Bortolami and Ballerini were bridging, and he took his chance. It did not matter; if they caught him they would say he was working for the team, and if he stayed away they would call him a champion. It was a good move.

The break slowly brought Tafi back, but then Bortolami and Ballerini had bridged, the two went straight to the front, and you could see the others shift gears and sprint to hold their wheels as the speed suddenly increased. Tafi swung onto the last wheel and coasted for a moment to recover, and then he went back up to the front and began working with Bortolami. These two riders drove the break; Bortolami drawn forward on the saddle with his face desperate, Tafi long and low over the bicycle with his face showing nothing.

How much time do they have, I wondered. They showed them from above on the long straight road you could see the break ahead surrounded by cars and motors, and the peloton behind in the distance. I chose a farmhouse on the side of the road and began counting as the break passed, and when the peloton reached the farmhouse they had twenty seconds. That is very close, I thought. Motorola, Gan, and Lotto were chasing hard, and there was the tension with the small gap and the two groups. Yates, Duclos-Lassalle, and Tchmil attacked off the front, but with each attack Museeuw brought the peloton back together. He rode in second or third position, watching the others, jumping onto each wheel, following behind until the rider slowed. He was a real champion; there were not many riders who could control the peloton, and there were not many leaders who would work for their team.

There was also the rivalry between Museeuw and Tchmil. Once they had been teammates. Then, at the world championships in 1993, Tchmil, riding for his own country and not his trade team, refused to help Museeuw chase down the American Lance Armstrong who had broken away alone. Armstrong took Worlds and Museeuw promised that Tchmil would never win a race again. That spring in Paris-Roubaix, when Tchmil attacked, Museeuw chased in a light rain over the pavé, closing to within eight seconds, before slowing and dropping back. Tchmil won, and now Museeuw would not let any rider break away. As they crossed the motorway between Lille and Brussels the time gap began to grow; first it was thirty seconds, then forty, then fifty. When the gap went over one minute the team cars came up, and I knew they would stay clear to Roubaix.

The break came onto sector five between Templeuve and Pont-Thibaut. Bortolami and Tafi were working on the front, and Dietz, Echimov, and Vanderaerden were following behind. Ballerini was riding at the back of the line and you could see him resting and shaking out his legs before they reached the town. Then he switched his hands to the drops, shifted gears, jumped on the pedals and attacked. The first motor followed and he went down the dusty yellow cobbled road and turned onto the smooth gray paved roads through Pont-Thibaut. He had broken away. There were twenty miles left to Roubaix.

The second motor picked up the peloton on sector five. They were racing down the pavé with the heavy crowds on the sides, the cars and bicycles along the ditch, and the sun warm and clear and high above the dust. Ahead there were stands of bare brown trees, a few pink flowering bushes, and Pont-Thibaut where Ballerini was racing through the streets alone. The motor dropped back through the peloton, and suddenly you saw Duclos-Lassalle riding slowly on the right of the road with his arm raised and the flat rear wheel of his bicycle sliding over the pavé. The peloton streamed past, the first cars in the caravan, the small groups of riders working their way forward, and then Duclos-Lassalle looked back and skidded to a stop and swung off the bicycle.

A motor had stalled on the pavé blocking the road and the caravan was stopped behind. Duclos-Lassalle pounded his fist on the saddle and waved his arms and shouted at the driver of the motor, but you could not hear his shouts over the sound of the crowd and the honking horns and the helicopter, and there was only his mute contorted face covered with brown dust, his mouth moving silently, and his eyes following the other riders as they passed. The crowd closed over Duclos-Lassalle and the photographers crouched in the road shooting him, and he removed the rear wheel from his bicycle and waved it high over his head signaling the team car. Finally the cars backed up and drove around through the fields and the caravan began moving. The Gan car arrived, the mechanic was out of the car running, the wheel was quickly changed, and Duclos-Lassalle was back on the bicycle sprinting down the road.

This is probably one of the last times Duclos-Lassalle will ride Paris-Roubaix, I thought. Soon he would retire. I remembered when he won Paris-Roubaix for the first time in '92, standing on the podium with his arms raised and his proud old smiling face. He came off sector five into Pont-Thibaut. The streets were empty and the dust was blowing away over the fields and the crowd was walking back along the sides of the road. They will not recognize him now, I thought. He is just another rider in the caravan. Maybe he would catch them. Maybe he would win for a third time. You could never tell at Paris-Roubaix. Duclos-Lassalle disappeared through the streets of Pont-Thibaut, racing after the peloton.

The first motor picked up Ballerini on the road. The gap was under one minute, the team car had not yet come up, and he was alone. They showed him from the side with his big solid body low on the bicycle, his jersey blown flat in the wind, and his head raised looking down the road. At the bottom of the screen the screen were the words tete de la course. Ballerini came onto sector four at Boughelles and raced straight down the pavé, the bicycle bouncing and shaking, his arms tensing, his thick muscular legs turning over with powerful surging strokes. Then he reached the road and passed the first sign for Roubaix, and you saw the white placard with the green La Redoubte, the distance remaining, 24 kilometers, and the word ARRIVÉE, finish. He drank, spit to clear the dust from his mouth, and leaned back down over the bicycle.

What was he thinking? Could he feel the ache in his shoulders and the numbness in his hands and the pain in his legs? Was he concentrating on his breaths and the rhythm of the gear? Was he counting down the sectors to Roubaix: sector three at Camphin-en-Pevele, eighteen kilometers; sector two at Gruson, fourteen kilometers; sector one at Hem, six kilometers. Probably he was thinking of coming into the velodrome alone. Ballerini had never won a Classic. He had come very close; seventh at Milan-San Remo, sixth at Flanders, third at Liège, second at Paris-Roubaix. That year Ballerini pulled Duclos-Lassalle all the way to Roubaix. Duclos-Lassalle was very experienced on the track and raced the indoor Six Days in the winter. When they came into the velodrome Ballerini was leading, and then, on the last lap, Duclos-

Lassalle moved to the front. In the final corner Ballerini tried to pass, but Duclos-Lassalle took him up the steep track, and they came off the banks, raced shoulder to shoulder down the straight, and threw their bicycles over the line. Ballerini believed he won and rode a victory lap with his arm raised. Then they showed the tape of the finish and you saw that Duclos-Lassalle had crossed the line first. Ballerini promised that he would never come back to Paris-Roubaix, but now he was racing alone at the front.

The cars and motors came up and Ballerini was surrounded on the road. He dropped back to the team car and you saw Fernandez leaning half-out the window driving with one hand and shouting and banging on the side of the car, and Lefevre and the mechanic cheering as well. The gap showed at 1:25. Ballerini went back to the front and the cars and motors closed around him.

The second motor picked up the chase group between Ballerini and the peloton. The Mapei-GB car had passed on ahead and the other cars had been pulled. Dietz, Echimov, and Vanderaerden were working on the front, and Tafi and Bortolami were following behind. Then, from the back of the line, Tafi attacked. Again you saw him jump on the pedals and sprint down the road, again you saw him lean forward over the bicycle, again you saw him settle into the high steady pace. He is attacking to drop the others, I thought. There was still a chance they would catch Ballerini. Vanderaerden had once won Paris-Roubaix, and Echimov was one of the best track riders in the peloton. Echimov slowly pulled Tafi back, leaning low over the bicycle as if he were riding a pursuit race on the track, and Dietz and Vanderaerden were dropped. As soon as Echimov caught Tafi, Bortolami attacked, and when Echimov caught Bortolami, Tafi attacked. Tafi and Bortolami attacked over and over, one after the other, and Echimov chased down each attack. Finally, broken by the Mapei-GB riders, Echimov sat up and slowed.

At the back of the line Bortolami stood on the pedals to stretch his legs and looked back down the road. The peloton was just behind. The three moved to the side, the motors passed, and the break that had been at the front since the Arenberg was caught.

There were close to thirty riders in the peloton. Yates, Tchmil, Museeuw, and Duclos-Lassalle. Tafi, Bortolami, and Echimov. Dietz, Vanderaerden, and Capiot. The Canadian Steve Bauer and the American George Hincapie. The Belgian John Claude Colotti, the old rider Adri van der Poel, and a young rider named Jarno showing well in his first Paris-Roubaix. The sprinters Fabio Baldato of MG-Technogym, Rolf Aldag of Deutsche Telekom, Wilifred Nelissen of Lotto wearing the red-black-yellow jersey of the Belgian national champion, and Fredric Moncasin of Novell who had won Kuurne-Brussels-Kuurne in February. They were the riders left of the almost two hundred-strong peloton that had started that morning in the Place du General de Gaul in Compeigne. It was afternoon and they were riding through a forest of widely spaced trees, with the clear yellow sun falling through the trees illuminating the bright colors of the peloton, and the cloud of brown dust lifting from the road. They came off the pavé and passed the ten kilometer sign for Roubaix.

Ballerini reached sector one at Hem. The gap stood at 1:35. He had slowed and they showed him from the side with his shoulders swaying back and forth, his mouth open breathing hard, and his cheeks drawn back in a grimace. Don't give up now, I thought. Not when you're so close. Ballerini switched to the paved path on the bank, reached down for his bottle, drank the last of the water, opened his hand, and let the bottle blow away behind. He won't need that anymore, I thought. There were still green and brown fields on the sides and woods beyond, but in the distance you could see the motorway and the low white industry on the outskirts of Roubaix. When he came off the pavé there was only the run through the city to the velodrome.

Ballerini came off the last sector of pavé into the streets of Roubaix. He rode under the five kilometer banner and passed the parked cars and rows of brick and slate houses, the crowds growing larger as he raced toward the center of the city, and then he reached the long straight boulevard with the rows of trees, barricades on the sides, and flags overhead. The cars and motors were following, the crowd was cheering, and you could see the La Redoute and television placards and the one kilometer banner ahead. He passed under the one kilometer banner, turned right, and they pulled the cars and followed him for as long as they could with the motors. Then they switched to the fixed cameras, and you saw him racing through the curves, shaking his head as if he did not believe it. In front of him was the high white velodrome, and you could hear the crowd chanting his name as he approached.

Ballerini swept onto the track and a great roar went up from the crowd. There were the stands crowded with people, the high banked track white in the sun, and the flat green infield. Around the track were the circling black, red, and blue lines, the La Redoute and television placards, the standing red Coca-Cola meter markers, the swept dirt apron, and the tents and podium on the infield. There were two laps of the track before the finish, and Ballerini sprinted down the backstretch into the shadows of the third and fourth corners, and rounded into the bright sun on the straight. His face was covered with brown dust, and he was smiling and shaking his fist over his head. He came down the straight with the announcer shouting in French and the crowd chanting his name and the bell ringing for the last lap, and he passed the finish and went back around the track, looking small at the bottom of the banks, with the colorful swaying swelling movement of the crowd following him in the stands. He raced down the backstretch and rounded onto the straight, sat up and kissed his hands and raised them to the crowd, and finally smoothed his jersey, lifted his arms in a wide salute, and rolled slowly across the line shaking his head.

Tchmil lead the peloton into Roubaix and down the boulevard toward the velodrome. He rode down that same boulevard once alone, I thought, in the rain, covered with black mud, the crowd chanting his name. As Tchmil passed the crowd cheered because they remembered his victory, and because Tchmil now lived in Roubaix and they considered him Belgian. Behind the peloton was massing for the sprint. They passed the one kilometer banner and turned toward the velodrome, and when the fixed cameras picked them up Bortolami was racing on the front.

Suddenly they were on the track sprinting down the backstretch and the great roar went up from the crowd. Bortolami was leading, and behind you could see Museeuw, Echimov, and Tchmil. They rode into the shadows of the third and fourth corners, rounded into the sun, and came off the banks past the finish with the announcer shouting and the crowd cheering and the bell ringing for the last lap. Look at them racing, I thought. After one-hundred-sixty-five miles they were sprinting for the finish; the pure sprinters would not be able to touch them at that distance, and the fight was among the leaders for World Cup points. Bortolami led out the sprint around the first and second corners, Museeuw came through looking back over his shoulder, and then they were all out of the saddle sprinting down the backstretch, with the peloton bunched behind in a small group at the bottom of the track. As they came into the shadows of the last corners Museeuw took the inside line, leaning down pushing hard into the banks, Tchmil began to pass on the outside, and Echimov came over the top and dove down the track. They rounded into the sun and spread out on the straight, racing shoulder to shoulder with their heads down, and they gathered themselves, lunged forward, and threw the bicycles over the line.

Tchmil took the sprint for second place. Museeuw was third. Echimov was fourth. Capiot won the bunch sprint for fifth. That was small consolation, I thought; if Capiot had not been dropped the whole race might have changed. In bicycle racing there was not only the winner, there were also the riders who made the breaks, the riders who led the long pursuits, the riders who took the bunch sprints, and the riders who simply played a part during the important moments of the race. There were as many stories and small races within the races as there were riders in the pack, but you had to know about the sport to understand the lesser dramas, and that was why it was difficult to appreciate on television, or even as a spectator standing beside the road.

The others came into the velodrome in small groups or alone, slowly circling the track, the crowd cheering. They crossed the line and slumped over the bicycles, or turned across the apron and rode onto the infield and collapsed in the grass, immediately surrounded the team personnel, photographers, and reporters.

Ballerini was on the podium for the victory ceremony. He was wearing a clean new Mapei-GB jersey and Mapei-GB cap, and somebody had wiped his face and placed a can of Coca-Cola in his hand. Jean-Marie Leblanc was standing on the side, the sponsors in suits were smiling and clapping, and the photographers were kneeling on the infield. They gave Ballerini the trophy of the small paving stone set on a marble base, he held the trophy over his head, the crowd cheered, the sponsors clapped, and the photographers shot him from below. Ballerini stepped down from the podium. I was glad that he won his race. Ballerini deserved to win Paris-Roubaix, if there was such a thing as "deserved" in sports.

The coverage ended and I turned away from the television. My hands were damp with sweat and my heart was pounding and I felt drained and hollow. There was the faint sad feeling after the race. It was always that way; you got caught up in the emotions and then it was over. I had spent the whole day watching Paris-Roubaix. The bar was empty and there were people passing on the avenue. The bartender was standing at the end of the counter.

"Is it finished?"

"Until the summer—then there's the Tour." In the summer the Tour lasted three weeks. Every day I would come up to the bar to watch the race. For a moment I thought of the summer, how the long days would run together with the races on the weekends, how dreams of the Tour would run in my head while I trained and raced, how the whole season would be subsumed by the Tour. I stood from the counter and went out into the bright sun on the avenue. It was warm and you could smell the country on the wind blowing down from the hills. I crossed the avenue and turned under the trees walking back toward the apartment.

10

A few weeks after Paris-Roubaix we drove north to Marin, left the populated suburbs behind, came over the grassy rolling hills and oak country into the Sonoma Valley. In Santa Rosa we turned off the highway onto a smaller road, and arrived at the small town where there was the Santa Rosa road race.

The race ran down into the valley through the vineyards and fields and came back over the hills toward the finish. On the second to last lap we turned out of the hills onto the long straight. I was riding in the middle of the pack, my jersey open, my body covered with sweat, my legs aching faintly after the fifty miles we had completed since morning. I was tired, but I still felt strong, and I knew that if I finished with the first group I could place in the race. Ahead was the feedzone with the people standing in rows on the hill and the banner over the crest. I reached down and drank the last of my water, threw the empty bottle into the fields, and moved to the side of the pack. Then we were on the hill climbing fast with the loud cheers and shouts and sound of running feet, I swung my arm backward, one of the feeders swung their arm forward, and as we passed our hands met and the water bottle slapped heavy and full onto my palm. I drank quickly, stood on the pedals, and went over the crest of the hill.

On the descent the pack spread out and I sat up with my hands on the brake hoods looking over the country. The hills spread down to the wide green valley, with the lines of the vineyards and the burnt yellow fields below, and the white spread of Santa Rosa in the distance. It was sunny and warm and the wind was coming up the valley moving the grass and making the air hazy and thick. The road ran out on the flats and the pack came back together into a large group. I leaned down over the bicycle and began moving toward the front.

When we reached the hills the pack was stretched in a line driving hard. I was riding near the front, and ahead I could see the first of the climbs. As we came onto the hill the front slowed and I shifted down through the gears keeping steady pressure on the pedals. Then, from several places back, one rider attacked and jumped away. Two others dove from the pack and caught his wheel, and they went up the hill one-two-three in line, with their bicycles swinging back and forth, their legs driving down in unison, and their backs crowned with sun.

The three riders quickly gapped the group and went over the crest of the hill. In the pack the first riders fell back and I came through on the front pushing hard to keep the gear turning on the grade. Looking back over my shoulder I saw the line broken apart on the climb. John was coming up the line and the others were farther behind. We crested the hill and the break already looked small on the road racing in the dip between the hills. I had hoped the race would stay together for the sprint, and I did not want to work before the finish, but at that moment, having missed the break, having placed in no races, and having gotten no points, I knew that I had to attack. Once they disappear the pack will not chase, I thought. The longer you wait the harder it will be to get across. I knew that if I wanted to make the break I had to attack.

I jumped on the pedals and sprinted away from the pack with the sudden open feeling on the road and the rising wind and hard resistance of the gear. When I gained speed I let the bicycle come forward beneath me and sat down, leaning over the handlebars with my head down, my back flat and low, and my legs spinning. I could feel other riders on my wheel and I moved to the side of the road where there was no cross-draft and pushed harder. Slowly they faded behind. Ducking my head I looked back under my arm; the pack was cresting the hill and there were a few riders spread out on the descent. You have a gap, I thought. You broke away. Now you have to give it everything and not look back and bridge to the break as fast as you can.

The road ran out between the hills and the spin of the descent slowly changed to the steady driving of the flats. Think of motorpacing, I said to myself. Think of motorpacing behind the car with Anne. I wish she was here now. Well, she isn't. You are alone. You will make the break and place in the race, or you will be caught by the pack. My breaths were coming faster and the solid internal ache was spreading upward from my legs as I worked into the wind coming over the fields. Leaning down over the bicycle I smoothed my pedaling, pulled myself forward on the saddle, and looked back up the road.

The break was onto the second hill with the riders climbing out of the saddle in line. No, I thought, they can't be that far away; it was just a trick with the two hills and the dip in the road. But I knew that it was not a trick and there was still a large gap to close. I came onto the hill and shifted down through the gears, and the steady driving of the flats faded into the slow push of the climb. My breaths were fast and high and my heart was racing and the pain was growing in my legs. Come on, I said to myself, don't give up now. This is the hardest part. I slid back in the saddle and pulled harder on the handlebars and drove down on the pedals. Just keep working, I thought. Soon it will be over. When you come over the crest of the climb it will all be downhill.

Looking up I saw the break cresting of the hill. They were closer and I stood on the bicycle and leaned all of my weight on each stroke forcing the pedals around. Finally my legs were unsteady and I sat down and slowed. My breaths were heaving and my heart was pounding and there was the hot spreading weakness over my body. Everything was dulled and distant, and I stared at the road under the front wheel. I had given up but I did not care. Slowly I ground forward over the crest of the hill. On the descent I gained speed and raised my head. I had crossed to the break.

When I drew onto the last wheel of the break I sat up and coasted. The rider coming down the line looked back and swung in front of me, and I reached down and drank, the water warm in the bottle but clear and cool down my throat and through my body. You made it, I thought. You made the break. Now you have to hold on until the finish and place in the sprint. I sat out one rotation at the back of the line to recover, and then I shifted gears and went up the line to the front.

The break was working smoothly. I came through and pulled into the wind and dropped back. I did not know any of the others and they all seemed to be from different teams. That's good, I thought. The others will not chase and we have a chance of staying away to the finish. The motor came up and the official shouted the time check over the sound of the engine; we had forty seconds. I moved into the draft and went back up the line.

Riding in the break there was the steady driving pace and smooth rotation and feeling of working together with the others. In the crosswinds we formed echelons, on the downhills we rotated faster, pulling off hard and slinging forward, and on the uphills we climbed out of the saddle to keep the speed high. It was different than riding in the pack; there was not the careful guarded feeling holding yourself back waiting to place, and I was happy to be at the front making the race in the break.

As we came down from the hills I could see the open green country in the valley. When I stood on the pedals there was a slow cramp in my thighs and I sat down and resumed pedaling. Hold on, I thought, you're almost there. Soon you'll turn onto the straight for the final climb. Ducking my head I looked back down the road. The pack was coming over the crest of the last hill with the long line and the tight bunched mass at the front chasing hard. I reached down, drank the last of my water, threw the bottle away, and looked back up the road.

Before the last turn the motor passed and accelerated toward the finish. The gap had come down and the pack was closing fast. We moved to the outside, banked through the turn, and came upright on the straight. Far ahead I could see the hill with the banner and the finish. The wind was blowing from behind and we flattened into line on the side of the road. The two riders at the front pulled off and dropped back, and the third came through on the front. You cannot lead out the sprint into the wind, I thought. You have to hold wheels and wait for the others to jump. Looking back I saw the pack turn the corner and spread out on the straight, with the riders on the front standing on the pedals and sprinting. They looked far away but I knew they were close, and I turned around and did not look back again.

Coming down the straight I rode with my head turned slightly to the side watching the two behind, their shadows on the road, the rider ahead, and the finish drawing closer. When would they jump? I wished I knew them. The big one was the only one who looked like he had a sprint. He was riding for an out-of-district team from San Diego, and he was perfectly placed at the back of the line, looking not directly at but over the break and the straight and the finish. The first rider was racing into the wind, his head down, his body low over the bicycle, his legs driving round. He had no chance of winning but he had committed himself to the front and there was no time to change position now. Finally he shifted gears, stood on the pedals, and began to lead out the sprint.

The finish was closer and you could see the faces of the crowd and the banner at the top of the hill. The first rider slowed, and there was the lack of speed and tension waiting to sprint. Come on, I thought. The pack is going to catch you. You have to go now. I stood on the pedals and began to swing the handlebars back and forth bringing the high gear up to speed. It was too early and I knew that I would never make it all the way, but I had to go and hold on as long as I could. Maybe I would reach the line.

Then out of the corner of my eye I saw the shadow of the big rider jump on the road as he attacked from behind, and I jumped hard and dove to the side and caught his wheel as he swept past. Pulling onto the wheel I narrowed my body in the draft with the wind rushing and the sides blurring. We came onto the hill and the gear was suddenly heavy and I pushed harder, throwing the handlebars back and forth and driving down on the pedals. Slowly my momentum built and there was the fast swinging rhythm of the bicycle and my weight coming down on each stroke and the surging feeling of speed. I dropped back slightly from the wheel ahead, shifted into the last gear, and sprinted up through the draft and around into the wind, not feeling the pedals, not feeling the pain in my legs, racing shoulder to shoulder up the climb.

We had almost reached the finish when there was a building sound from behind and a flash of color as the pack came over in a driving line. No, I thought, not so close to the finish. The pack passed and I sat down and coasted with my hands in the drops and my head raised looking up the road. They spread out with the riders at the front sprinting and there was the final surge and bunched throw as they crossed the line. I came over the crest and under the banner.

On the descent I coasted. My breaths were heaving and my heart was pounding and my body was racing from the sprint. Again you did not place, I thought. Again the race is over and you did not get any points. Why didn't you go earlier? You knew they were close and you had nothing to lose. The first rider was the only one who deserved to place, I thought. He went straight to the front and raced as hard as he could for the finish.

Slowly the wind built and the air grew warmer as I came down into the valley. At least you tried, I told myself. You attacked, bridged, and worked in the break. There was no way you could have gone from that far out and held them off in the wind, and you almost took the sprint anyway. The pack caught you at the line. That was racing. It was better not to think about it. Better to start thinking about the next race. Better to start thinking about the criterium tomorrow.

The road ran out in the valley and I sat up and shifted into a lighter gear. In the distance I could see the vineyards and the fields in the warm afternoon sun. Behind was the high forested ridge that led over to the coast. I rode along the hills until my body recovered and the feeling came back into my legs, and then I turned around and started back toward the cars to meet the others.

11

The criterium course in Santa Rosa started in a park, wound through narrow sidestreets, and came back on wide open streets to the finish. It was very technical and required great concentration. There was an early break and the pace was fast. I rode in the middle of the pack waiting to recover from the race the day before. As we raced the fatigue slowly disappeared, and with two laps to go the break had been caught, the pack was all together, and I was near the front. We came down the straight with the crowd cheering and the announcer shouting and the music playing, and over the other sounds I heard the ringing of the bell; there was the sudden rush through my body, and we swept past the finish and began the last lap.

In the first corner I leaned down and banked over the road, with the push of the bicycle and the hard resistance on the outside leg and inside arm, looking ahead keeping my eyes fixed on one point as the pack mixed and flowed in the background. We swung wide and came upright and sprinted down the straight.

You have to move up, I told myself. You can't wait until the finish. Pulling off I sprinted up the line and drew even with the front. I was riding into the wind but it was better than being trapped in the pack. The line swung to the outside and I moved into the draft sweeping another rider from the wheel ahead. When we banked into the next corner the rider leaned against me with his shoulder. I pushed back hard, he braked sharply and dropped back, and we rounded onto the backstretch.

At the front it was fast and smooth with all the riders low over the bicycles and wind rushing and the open feeling on the sides. We raced through the narrow streets and swung to the outside, and then suddenly the pack massed forward and slowed, and there was the tight-bunched trapped feeling with nowhere to move. For a moment two riders drifted apart and I jumped on the pedals and sprinted through the narrow gap. Then the pack rushed into the next corner, and I heard shouts and squealing brakes and the building scraping sounds of a crash.

There were always crashes on the last laps with everybody fighting for position. I thought of the crashes in the middle of the pack where you fell with the others in a great pile, the crashes where you came around a corner sweeping too wide trying to brake and lean away, the crashes where you suddenly found yourself on the ground trying to make yourself small as the pack rushed past in the road. It was part of racing, but you never grew accustomed to crashes, and when you heard the sounds there was an inward tensing fear and you braced yourself and raced faster.

The crash swept through the pack and we rounded the corner and came onto the straight that led back to the finish. I was filled with a sudden powerful relief having made it past the crash. Looking up I counted the riders ahead: I was in tenth position. I knew the pack was broken apart from the crash and that now, on the last lap, there was no way they could come around. You can place, I thought. You can place in this race. When I realized that I could place all the fatigue in my body disappeared and there was the sudden dry-mouthed tension and building excitement for the sprint. The line moved to the outside, I sat up for a moment and shook out my legs, and we banked over the road and dove into the final corner.

As soon as we swept onto the straight I looked up toward the finish. There was the wide open road with the great crowd behind the barricades and the banner in the distance. The wind was blowing down the course and I knew the sprint would be hard and that you could not go from a long way out. The first rider stood on the pedals and dove over the road with the line snaking behind like a whip cracking, and I pulled myself forward in the draft and shifted up through the gears holding myself back fighting the desire to sprint. Gradually the first rider slowed, the second came through on the front, and they were all sprinting with their heads down and their elbows out and the bicycles going from side to side.

We came into the barricades. I stood on the pedals and began to swing the handlebars back and forth bringing the bicycle up to speed. Wait, I told myself. Wait until you can see the finish. The crowd was cheering louder and I could hear the announcer shouting over the music. Finally I dropped back from the wheel ahead, shifted into the last gear, and jumped hard, coming up through the draft and around into the wind, with the final flat-out release of control and commitment of the sprint. Slowly the gear that had been heavy smoothed and became even and built with the fast swinging rhythm. I moved over against the barricades so that those behind could only pass on one side and drew even with the first riders. Beside me I could hear their labored breathing and the tires on the road and the wind rushing past. Then I was drawn forward over the front wheel and my arms and legs were weak and there was the desperate spun-out burning feeling of fatigue. The banner spread over the straight and I gathered my body, bent my arms and legs, and threw the bicycle over the line.

Sweeping under the banner I looked up and immediately counted the riders ahead: one, two, three—I had placed fourth. When I saw that I had finally placed there was a surge of relief and the tension drained away. You placed, I thought. I wonder what the prize will be? Probably a small check or a bottle of wine from one of the vineyards. I remembered how in Italy there were always prizes from the local shops, and how there were cups for the top ten and bouquets of flowers for the top three. But the prizes were not important; what was important were the points. Fourth place was worth three points. That was only a small part of what I needed to upgrade, but if I kept placing I could become a Category II before the end of the year. I did not really believe it was possible, but with the first points I began to hope distantly that I could ride with the professionals.

Thinking that I had finally placed and the season had truly begun I turned onto the backstretch away from the crowd. The pack was spreading out on the road and the Pro/I-IIs were coming onto the course. I was not tired and there was no pain in my legs, but I knew that later I would feel the fatigue from the weekend. I had raced fully both days and finally placed and earned my first points. The sun was shining and the sky was clear and there were a few high white clouds driven inland from the coast. I shifted into a lighter gear and rode back toward the finish, moving to the side as a driving line of Pro/I-IIs came past before their race.

12

In late spring I rode out from the trees along the ridge in the park. It was sunny and warm and below I could see the rolling green and brown hills around the reservoir. I coasted for a moment in the sun, and then leaned forward and went down the long descent into the country. When I reached the bottom of the descent I sat up and slowed, and instead of turning south along the highway, crossed the main road, dropped on the short descent, and rode straight into the hills.

The road flattened and began to climb above the reservoir in a long white curve. I shifted gears and settled into the steady pace. It was hot and I could feel my breaths coming faster and the sweat rising over my body. Slowly I rounded the curve, and there was the dam white in the sun, and the long straight leading into the hills shimmering in heat waves.

The Classics were over. Jalabert had taken Flèche-Wallone, and a Swiss rider had won Liège-Bastogne-Liège and Amstel Gold. Who are the famous Swiss champions? I wondered. Kubler and Koblet of the last generation, and now Rominger and Alex Zülle. Rominger and Zülle would be looking forward to the long stage races. Soon there would be the Four Days of Dunkirk and the Tour of Romandie, and then in May the first great three-week stage race of the year, the Tour of Italy, or Giro d'Italia.

This year the Giro would start in Perugia in the middle of Italy, I remembered. The first time trial would be in Assisi on stage two, and then they would race east to the coast and all the way down past

Pescara to Taranto in the south. Crossing the country the riders would come back up the west coast over Mount Sirino to Maddaloni for the second time trial, and continue north through Romagna and Veneto to Trento. On stage fourteen they would ride into the mountains to Val Senales, with the hillclimb time trial at Selvino in the Dolomites, and the stage to Briançon in the Alps, and then they would come into Milan for the finish. It was a good course; the large figure eight covered most of the country and there were enough mountains. It would be hot in the south and along the coasts, but there would still be snow and cold weather in the Dolomites. After the Giro there were the Midi Libre, the Dauphiné-Libéré, and the Tour of Switzerland, and then in July the Tour de France.

I crested the long false flat at the top of the climb and reached the descent. The slopes were tan and bare and covered with chaparral, and the road led down into the grassy open country. As I dropped on the road I thought about the Tour de France. It was the greatest bicycle race in the world. It was not just a race but a celebration of the whole country and the sport. Maybe Miguel Indurain would win again. He won the Tour four times, and if he won five he would match Merckx, Jacques Anquetil, and Hinault. What about Tony Rominger or Zülle or even Bugno? It would be wonderful to see Bugno win. In 1991 he was second in the Tour and in 1992 he was third. Last year he took Flanders, and early in the spring he won the Tour of the Med, but he was not the Bugno who lead the 1990 Giro from start to finish, won the world championships two years running with a long powerful sprint, and took Milan-San Remo and San Sebastian. Indurain defeated him in the Tour, defeated him in the Giro, and defeated him in all the other races for the rest of his career, first Bugno and Chiappucci, and now Rominger and Zülle. There were others: Evgeny Berzin, Jalabert, Marco Pantani, Richard Virenque. But I did not think that they could defeat Indurain.

At the bottom of the descent the road ran out in the fields and curved away through the hills. A smaller road turned right and led onto a short climb. The climb wound up through a forest with warm shade and broken yellow light through the pines along the road. Standing on the pedals I swept around the first corner, and then sat down and slid back in the saddle pushing against the grade, my breaths steady and deep, my body working over the bicycle with smooth fluid driving rhythm. I had been riding every day, my body was lean and strong from training, and my skin was burned brown from the sun. I knew that I was riding well going into the summer.

The road came out from the trees over the crest of the hill and I slowed looking down at the country. Below was the small forested valley around the town of Lafayette, and the highway leading back toward Oakland. I went down toward the town, dropping with the plunging rush on the steep road, sweeping through the gradual curves, and running out in the valley. It was the middle of the season. I was looking forward to the races. It was time. It was time for me to upgrade to Pro/I-II.

13

On the day of the Berkeley criterium Anne and I went up to the course together. She walked on the sidewalk and I rode slowly alongside, pedaling and coasting, my jersey open, my shorts and sleeves rolled up in the sun, my helmet hanging from the handlebar. It was a bright sunny day and the sky was clear blue. We came up past the campus, crossed Telegraph Avenue, and reached the course on the streets that sloped into the hills.

It was strange to see the city transformed for the race; the streets were blocked with barricades, there was an official platform, announcing stand, and banner over the straight, music was playing from the stands, and the sidewalks and cafe where we met for rides were crowded with people. We went up through the crowd to the cafe, found a table shaded by trees on the outside terrace, and sat down to watch the Category IV race.

It would be the first bicycle race Anne had ever seen. The pack rounded the course and came up the hill, flashing past the cafe with the sudden cheers and bright colors and smooth rushing speed. Anne watched with a serious expression, her eyes following the riders.

"It's so fast! How do you keep from falling?"

"We're all mixed together going the same speed."

"It's like a great noisy colorful parade."

The pack turned onto the backstretch and disappeared, and we sat at the table listening to the cheers on the other side of the course. When they came back around the bell rang for the last lap, and they raced up the hill and swept past in a driving line. The crowd cheered and all the people on the terrace got up and walked to the straight to watch the finish. I sat at the table with Anne. Look at her, I thought. She was wearing a sleeveless blouse and medium length skirt, her long brown hair made almost blond by the sun was swept back from her shoulders, her skin was dark brown, and she was very beautiful. At that moment I did not want to race. I thought of the summer, and all the races still ahead that year, and I knew that I would only become more and more absorbed in the season. You don't have to race, I thought. You could stay with Anne and watch the criterium and cheer for the others. You don't have to race at all. Don't think that way, I told myself. That's only before the race. You are afraid you will not place. It's spring and you're riding well. Of course you will race.

We heard the cheers approaching, and then there was the shout as the pack rounded the final corner, and they raced up the hill and crossed the line. The riders spread out on the road, and the others waiting on the sides ducked under the barricades and rode onto the course. I stood and buckled on my helmet, and Anne put her arms around me and kissed me on the mouth.

"I love you," she said. I held her close feeling her body pressed against mine and her head on my shoulder, and I stroked her hair and spoke into her ear.

"I love you, Anne."

"Good luck."

Turning away I took my bicycle and walked across the terrace to the sidewalk. I looked back, squinting in the bright sun, and saw Anne standing by the table. I grinned and waved and ducked under the barricades onto the straight.

We started facing the hills and turned the first corner past the cafe. The pack spread out on the road and we rounded onto the backstretch. From the top of the hill you could see the whole bay spread out below, with the water shining in the sun and San Francisco showing clearly. At the bottom of the hill was the wide open corner leading back toward the finish. Slowly we gained speed, and I leaned down over the bicycle and shifted up through the gears. Before the corner the line moved to the outside, and then we dove into the corner and swung wide, and I jumped on the pedals and sprinted up the short straight, stopped pedaling for a moment to lay the bicycle down, and rounded the final corner. The crowd cheered and we came up the hill and swept through the finish. As we passed the cafe I looked up from the pack, but I could no longer see Anne in the crowd. We went down the straight under the trees and turned onto the backstretch.

On the second lap two riders attacked off the front and moved clear. Knowing the criterium could finish with a break I went to the front and pulled hard in the wind, and then another rider attacked from behind, and when I saw that it was Dave I sat up and rode the brakes on the downhill so that he could get away. When we came back around the course Dave had bridged, and they went up the hill and turned the corner and disappeared. I hope they stay away, I thought. Dave has a good chance in the sprint and there are still three more places. It was too early to tell about the break, and I dropped back and moved into the pack.

I had raced the Berkeley criterium many times. Sometimes it finished with a break and sometimes the pack stayed together and it finished with a sprint. There was the year when it rained and most of the pack crashed in the corners. I went to the front and rode hard to stay warm and broke away with three others. Then there was the year when I was not riding well and I was dropped on the hill. I raced alone until I was so far behind that the pack was about to catch me and the officials pulled me from the race. In one of the corners I simply went straight and rode home. Now you are racing here again, I thought. The break has gone, Dave is ahead, and you can wait for the sprint.

By the middle of the race the break had reached the other side of the course and you could hear the distant cheers as they passed the finish. Then, slowly, the pack began to chase harder. They sprinted up the hill, worked in fast rotation on the downhill, and stretched the pack into a line, and the gap started to close. When they showed the lap cards with ten to go the break came back into sight; with five to go you could see them ahead on the straights keeping close to the barricades; finally with two to go the first rider in the line drew onto the last wheel of the break, pulled around, and sprinted past, and we swept over them in a driving line. As we passed I looked up and saw Dave dropping back, and we crested the hill and turned onto the backstretch.

You have to get to the front, I thought. You cannot wait until the last lap. I sprinted up line and pushed into the rotation, and we raced down the hill and came back around the course. When we rounded the final corner the first rider swung wide and I came through on the front. Behind the pack was massing forward for the finish. You can't slow down, I thought. Keep the speed high. I led up the hill climbing fast out of the saddle with the empty straight and the open feeling and the crowd cheering loud. Listen to them cheer. This is your crowd, this is your city, and this is your race. I shifted gears and my legs took the gear driving down smoothly and I shifted again pushing harder. My body was working over the bicycle and my breaths were deep and full and there was the feeling of growing building strength. I knew it was one of the days when I could win any race.

We swept past the finish with the crowd cheering and the announcer shouting and the music playing, and over the other sounds I heard the high ringing of the bell. I sat down and pushed over the crest of the hill, and we went down the straight under the trees and turned onto the backstretch. There was the long empty downhill with the fast sweeping corner at the bottom. Ducking my head I looked back under my arm and saw the pack stretched into line on my wheel. They want you to lead out the sprint, I thought. They want you to lead so that they can come around at the finish. No, I said to myself, nobody is going to come around. You can win from behind and you can win from the front. On a day like today you can win from anywhere. You have to get the jump out of the corner and hold them off on the hill.

On the downhill I swung back and forth in wide curves so that nobody could pass, and then at the last moment I came upright in the gutter, quickly shifted gears, and banked steeply into the corner. There was the fast hurtling rush and the deep pushing lean, and I swung wide and jumped on the pedals and sprinted out of the corner. I came up the straight, stopped sprinting to lay the bicycle down, and rounded onto the hill.

When I swept around the final corner a cheer went up from the crowd and I saw the straight leading up the hill with the crowd on the sides, the bright colors in the sun, and the banner and finish at the crest. I had a gap and I moved toward the gutter so they could only pass on one side, and began sprinting. Slowly the rhythm built with deep swinging of the handlebars and the solid driving on the pedals and the bicycle surging forward, and I came into the barricades. Then the sides were blurring and there was the steady roar from the crowd and the finish was drawing closer. The others were close behind and I dropped my head and pushed harder, throwing the handlebars back and forth and forcing the pedals around with legs-dead, arms-weak, breath-heaving fatigue. Finally I looked up and saw the banner spreading over the straight, the sides were clear, and I sat up and raised my arms as I crossed the line.

I won, I thought. I won. Sweeping through the finish I turned onto the straight almost overshooting the corner. I looked back but Anne was not at the cafe and I turned onto the backstretch. How did you win? You went from the front and got the jump and held them off on the hill. I could almost not believe what I had done, and I stood on the pedals and sprinted for a few strokes and then sat down. It was what I had always dreamed of and now I had won the Berkeley criterium. I was not tired at all and there was no pain in my legs. I was filled with happiness.

On the downhill Dave rode alongside and smiled and clapped me on the back.

"You won! I couldn't see the sprint."

"I went from the corner."

"I knew when they caught you could win."

We coasted down the hill and I sat up and opened my jersey, feeling the warm sun and building wind on my face. Below the bay was shining in the sun and you could see the clear blue sky stretched all the way to the horizon. First place was worth several points. With the other points I had almost enough to upgrade and it was not even summer. John had upgraded, Dave would upgrade soon, and maybe Chris would move up as well, and we could all race together in the Pro/I-IIs. It was close now, and I was sure that I would upgrade before the end of the year.

Dave and I came back around the course and rode up the hill with the few cheers and light applause from the crowd. Then I saw John and Chris waiting by the barricades and Anne standing apart, and I pulled to the side and stopped over the bicycle.

"Anne!"

"You won!" She put her arms around me and kissed me on the mouth. "I couldn't see you with the others except at the beginning, and then suddenly you were at the front and you won!"

I took off my helmet and Anne handed me a bottle of water. I drank, and then poured the water over my head and shoulders washing away the sweat, and drank the rest of the bottle. John was about to start with the Pro/I-IIs. We watched the large pack gather on the straight, the official gave them the directions, and they moved off and disappeared around the first corner.

We waited for the official results, and then I picked up the prize of the small check and bouquet of flowers, shook hands with the director, and left the stand. I gave the flowers to Anne and we went down through the crowd and away from the race. She walked holding the flowers and I rode alongside holding her hand. I had won and we were together. It was a day I would remember for the rest of the season.

14

On July first I walked up to the bar to watch the prologue of the Tour de France. It was a bright sunny day and the avenue was crowded with people. The bar was empty and shaded, the windows and doors were open, and there was a light breeze blowing through from the avenue. The bartender remembered me from the spring, and he switched the television to the European sports channel. In France it was late evening. The sky was dark and it was raining. You could see the riders waiting on the starting platform with the rain coming down in lines, the wind blowing hard, and the huge crowd spread below in the glare of white and yellow lights. One by one the riders rolled down the ramp into the streets of St. Brieuc.

The prologue was really just a show before the race began. The next day they would start stage one from Dinan, and in the first week they would ride north and east through Brittany and Normandy into Belgium for the first long time trial. In the second week they would transfer by air to Geneva, ride into the Alps, cross central France, and enter the Pyrénées in the south. In the third week they would come down from the mountains to Bordeaux, and turn back toward Paris. The first Tour traveled from Paris, to Lyon, to Marseille, to Toulouse, to Bordeaux, to Nantes, to Paris. That was almost one hundred years ago. It all began because of the Dreyfus affair, a rich count, and a newspaper editor who wanted to sell more papers, but nobody remembered that now. Now the bicycle race took over France for twenty-three days in July. The Tour had its own president, police force, bank, villages, and population of four thousand workers who followed the race. It was really like another country, with land that included not only France but parts of Belgium and Germany, the Swiss and Italian Alps, the Pyrénées of Spain, famous cities like St. Etienne and Bordeaux, and streets like the Champs-Elysées in Paris.

I watched them racing in the yellow lights of the follow cars, and I thought of the feeling of the rain on their faces, the wet bars in their hands, their legs driving round. I hoped that they would all finish the prologue and make it to Paris.

Most of the riders knew the few seconds lost or gained in the short time trial would mean nothing after three weeks of racing, and they rode just fast enough to put on a show for the crowd, coming slowly down the ramp, braking before the corners, riding down the center of the roads. Others were not thinking of the second week or third weeks. They were thinking only of winning the prologue and taking the yellow jersey, and they sprinted down the ramp and raced hard through the streets in the rain, cutting the corners, sliding the wheels of their bicycles, keeping close to the barricades out of the wind.

When Chris Boardman came down the ramp you could see that he was racing for the yellow jersey. He had won the prologue the year before, and he had come to the Tour to win the prologue again. Because he was British I always liked too see him to do well, and I watched him sprint away through the streets of St. Brieuc. The motor picked him up on the road and you could see him low over the bicycle racing hard through the rain. Then, in a sweeping left hand corner, Boardman was suddenly on the ground, and he crashed into the metal barricades with the team car swerving to a stop. At the bottom of the screen the small window appeared with the name, Boardman, Chris, the words, *Chute,* crash, *Les Blessés,* the injured, and *Abandonner,* abandon. Boardman had crashed out of the Tour. They switched to the second motor and picked up another rider on the road.

That was how the Tour began. A Frenchman named Jacky Durand won the prologue. They showed him on the podium smiling and excited, pulling on the first yellow jersey. He rode for the Castorama team, and I remembered that he had taken the stage to Cahors the year before. The coverage ended and I looked away from the television. The bar was empty and people were passing in the street. I paid for my drink and went out of the darkened bar into the bright sun.

15

That afternoon I climbed above the city on my bicycle. It was sunny and bright and the sky was clear. I opened my jersey, rolled up my sleeves and shorts, and stood on the pedals on the steep road. When I rounded above the houses I could see the city glaring white below, the bay shining in the sun, and the coastal mountains shimmering in the heat. Slowly the city and bay grew smaller, and I reached the ridge and rode into the parks.

When I came over the ridge there was sudden sharp smell of summer; dry grasses, eucalyptus, pine, and dust from the valley. Looking down through the trees I could see the slopes covered with high brown waving grass, and the rolling brown hills around the reservoir. All the country that was green in the spring was now dry and brown and burned by the sun. In the distance was a long cloud of dust over the Great Central Valley. I could not see the Sierra.

The road came out from the trees and began the long descent, the air growing hotter, the sweat drying on my body. At the bottom of the hills I sat up and flared my arms, taking the blast of air against my chest, and then turned south along the highway. On the climb the trees were full and green and the branches formed a thick canopy over the road. Riding through the warm shade, my body working, the sweat running down my face, I thought of the Tour.

They had started racing now and would not stop for three weeks.

While I raced and ate and slept they would be on the road. Every day there would be a new stage, every stage there would be a new winner, and slowly the overall leader would emerge. All of the favorites were far back in the prologue: Indurain, Rominger, Zülle, Jalabert, Berzin, Pantani, Virenque. Maybe Durand would hold on for the first week. Castorama was a strong team. But then one of the others would take the yellow jersey.

The semester had finished and college was out for the summer. Anne and I were living together in Berkeley. She had gotten an internship in San Francisco and I was working for an English professor on campus. I saw her in the evenings, and most weeks I had time to train and race. Every day I went up to the bar to watch the Tour. It was the only time of year that I regularly watched sports, but it was the Tour de France.

Cresting the hill above Moraga I saw the houses in the heat and the steep canyons leading back to the city. I shifted gears, leaned forward over the bicycle, and went down into the town.

16

After the first stages they began to show the Tour in the evening. When I came up to the bar it was dark, there were people at the tables, and the bartender was working behind the counter. I sat down and the bartender switched on the television. We watched them start stage four in Alençon.

The Village Depart was set up in the town square. There were old stone buildings around the square, lines of blue-white-red French flags overhead, white tents for the Tour guests, and the great stage with the announcing stand where they signed on each day. On one side was the metal gantry with the Depart banner, and around the square were the signs of all the sponsors: red Coca-Cola, blue Fiat, 2-Sport-3 television, green PMU, red Champion, and yellow Credit Lyonnais. The square was crowded with people, and the peloton was grouped under the gantry on the road. Many of the riders were wearing long-sleeved jerseys and gloves and boots, and they looked cold waiting on the line for the start. The director conducted a short ceremony, the band played the French national anthem, the mayor cut the white tape, and the riders rolled forward as the crowd cheered.

The Tour was really like a story. First there was the prologue, then there was the introduction over the flat stages, the action took place in the mountains, and finally there was the conclusion and dramatic ending in Paris. It was a play in three acts: week one, week two, and week three. A great celebration.

They came through Alençon and spread out on the road in the country. The caravan for the Tour was much longer than for the Classics. At the front, far ahead of the peloton, were the special Garde Republicaine on motorcycles clearing the road. Then there was the line of publicity vehicles, the advance cars, and the red car with the placard and flashing lights of the race director, Jean-Marie Leblanc. Behind was the peloton, the long line of team cars, press cars, commisaire cars, service cars, medical cars, team buses, and the *voiture balai*, or broom wagon, which followed like a broom sweeping up the riders who had abandoned. Finally there were all the motors moving within the peloton, and the helicopters flying above and landing in the fields to refuel.

They had left Brittany and were riding up through Normandy and the Pays d'Auge toward the Atlantic coast. The country was green and rolling, with gentle hills and forests and fields, and you could see the plain stretched away under the heavy gray clouds. The helicopters were flying low under the clouds, and they showed the race from above, with the peloton stretched into the long line on the road. There were twenty-one teams in the Tour. Nine riders on each team made almost two-hundred riders in the peloton. There would not be that many when they finished in Paris. On the front you could see the pink jerseys of the ONCE team working for Jalabert. Over the last stages Jalabert had sprinted for all the intermediate time bonuses, taking the yellow jersey away from Durand. There had been an early break and ONCE was making the pace. As we watched, a rider sprinted down the road and moved clear. The bartender nodded at the screen.

"Are they trying to break away like before?"

"Yes, but this is only the fourth stage. The whole race is three weeks long." The Tour was harder to understand than the Classics. I told the bartender that you could think of each stage as a separate race, with a longer race for the overall. They timed the stages, and each rider was given a cumulative time for all stages covered. The rider with the lowest cumulative time was the overall leader, and wore the *maillot jaune*, or yellow jersey.

"Can you see the rider in yellow near the front? That's Laurent Jalabert. He's ahead by a few seconds so he's wearing the yellow jersey."

"Why's it yellow and not some other color like blue or white or red?"

I told the bartender how the first Tour was sponsored by *L'Auto* newspaper that was printed on yellow paper. Now *L'Auto* had become *L'Equipe*, but the jersey was still yellow. In Italy the Giro was sponsored by the *Gazzetta dello Sport*, printed on pink paper, so there was the *maglia rosa*, or pink jersey. In Spain in the Vuelta there was the *jersey de amarrillo,* but there was no yellow paper that I knew, and sometimes I heard it called the *jersey de oro,* or jersey of gold. The Giro and the Vuelta wonderful races, but they were not as great as the Tour.

"There's also a green jersey for the best sprinter and a red-and-white jersey for the best climber," I said. "All the races go on together, but the most important is the yellow jersey for the overall leader."

They came through the country and over the great bridge across the mouth of the Seine and down into Le Havre, with the dark green hills, white buildings, and flat gray sky. Mercatone-Uno and ONCE were leading out the sprint, and the early break had been caught. The motors picked them up under the five kilometer banner, and there were riders attacking on both sides. Mercatone-Uno and ONCE brought the peloton back together, and when they came down into the center of Le Havre Museeuw broke away alone. He raced through the streets, crested a small hill, and swept down to the Atlantic coast.

Along the coast the clouds had lifted and the sun was shining and there was a strong wind blowing off the water. Museeuw reached the waterfront and raced along the boulevard fronted by rows of old houses

and high white apartment buildings. On the other side were board-
walks, beaches with small white waves coming up on the shore, long
breakwaters, and the flat gray Atlantic.

The peloton reached the waterfront and stretched into a long line in
the wind. Lotto had come up leading out Wilfried Nelissen, and they
were working on the front with Mercatone-Uno and ONCE. Slowly
they brought Museeuw back, and then the peloton curved past a road
divider, and there was a crash. You saw the first rider look up from the
road, realize he was carrying too much speed, unclip from the pedals,
brace himself, and punch into the metal barricades, with the crowd
jumping back and the line driving into him from behind. The peloton
bunched and slowed, the riders streamed past on the sides, and then
they were back on the bicycles and the crowd closed over the barricades.
When the road cleared there was an MG-Technogym rider lying on his
back with his hands over his face, a Lotto rider on the curb, and another
standing with his bicycle. Then the words *Chute, Maillot Jaune,* came up
at the bottom of the screen, and I saw Jalabert in the road. They were
outside the one kilometer and would not give him the same time as the
others. He had lost the jersey. The team car came up, gave Jalabert a
new bicycle, and he got on the bicycle with the jersey scraped over his
shoulder and his shorts torn and bloody, and sprinted away down the
boulevard.

They picked up the peloton sweeping under the one kilometer
banner. There was no way the others would catch them now. There was
just the flat run to the finish and the great bunched pack sprint.
Mercatone-Uno was on the front leading out Mario Cipollini. He was
the best sprinter in the peloton. Tall and thin with a face like a model,
he paraded for the cameras, wore a different designer suit onto the
podium for each win, talked as much as he won, and always abandoned
the Tour in the mountains, after which they would find him relaxing

on the beach along the Riviera, but he had a long straight powerful sprint, and nobody could touch him on a flat wide open road. The only rider who came close was Djamolidin Abdujaparov from Uzbekistan, short and stocky, with sharp brown Asian features, a quiet personality, and a wild swerving sprint. He was not as fast as Cipollini, but was absolutely fearless, could handle the high mountains, and had won the green jersey three years running. There were others: Fabio Baldato, who had won the long drawn-out uphill sprint into Lannion on stage one, Jeroen Blijlevens, Nelissen, Eric Zabel, and Moncasin. As they came toward the finish all the teams massed forward forming the long leadout trains for the sprint.

The domestiques in the leadout trains pulled until they began to slow and then swung off and dropped back, and the riders behind came through racing as hard as they could. The peloton was stretched from one side of the road to the other, with the leadout trains at the front. From above the streaming lines looked smooth and fast, but I knew that inside there was the pushing, shoving, hand-slinging fight for position, with shouts, rubbing shoulders, and squealing brakes. Approaching the final corner they swung to the outside and you could see the water bottles jettisoned from the peloton like chaff to lighten the bicycles, and they split into two lines streaming around the slower riders in the middle of the road, and banked through the wide open corner onto the straight.

When they rounded the corner the wind picked them up from behind and swept them forward into a single line. Ahead was the long straight shadowed by old stone buildings, with the low red-and-white blocks funneling into the barricades, the 2-Sport-3 and red Coca-Cola boards, and the crowd leaning over the barricades cheering and shouting and waving small green flags. On the sides you could see the blue Fiat meter markers at 400 meters, 300 meters, 200 meters, 100 meters and 50 meters. Far down the straight, bright and hazy in the sun, was the finish.

The last Mercatone-Uno domestique sprinted down the straight with Cipollini on his wheel, and MG-Technogym rider on the barricades, and Zabel and Moncasin on the right and left. At four-hundred meters the Mercatone-Uno domestique swung off and dropped back, and Cipollini swerved over the road switching to the wheel of the MG-Technogym. Zabel stood on the pedals and began to sprint on the right, and Moncasin began to sprint on the left.

Cipollini was trapped behind the MG-Technogym. They passed the three-hundred meter mark, Zabel and Moncasin sprinting on the front, and still Cipollini was boxed-in behind. Then the MG-Technogym rider faded back on the right, and Cipollini jumped through the gap between Zabel and Moncasin. Now he'll begin to sprint, I thought. As every year Cipollini had won from the start of the season, taking stages at the Tour of the Med, the Tour of Valencia, Four Days of Dunkirk, and the Giro. He had already won stage two of the Tour at Vitre, and he was in line and only a little behind to win his second stage in Le Havre. They came into the last 200 meters with the announcer shouting and crowd cheering and swaying and waving along the straight. Zabel was driving hard on the pedals, Moncasin was looking up for the line, and Cipollini was sprinting smooth and straight and powerful with fast-building rhythm.

In the last hundred meters you could see the finish with the red metal gantry over the road, the white-and-black ARRIVÉE, the large red Coca-Cola banner, the great structure for the commisaires, the press boxes and guest stands, and the photographers standing in ranks all the way across the road shooting the sprint. They flashed past the fixed cameras and switched to the overhead swinging booms, and showed them from above in the last fifty meters. Zabel was drawn forward over the front wheel with his body jerking up and down, Moncasin was losing the rhythm of the sprint, and Cipollini was racing faster and faster, his long arms swinging the handlebars back and forth, his legs coming down solid and even on each stroke, the bicycle surging forward with a smooth fluid beautiful display of strength and speed. They passed the blue Fiat chevrons on the ground, the gantry spread over the straight, Zabel stopped sprinting, and Moncasin dropped his head and threw his bicycle forward. Cipollini sat up, clapped his hands over his head, and crossed the line in first place.

I leaned back from the counter and sat up at the bar. My heart was pounding and my hands were damp with sweat and my body was racing. Jalabert came down the straight leading a small group of riders, and crossed the line fifty seconds back. He had lost the yellow jersey. They showed the overall classification on the screen, and then the helicopter pulled away and you could see the old white city with the church spires, high apartment buildings, and dark green hills. Behind was the flat gray coast, clearing blue sky, and low white clouds moving away over the Atlantic. The coverage ended and I left the bar.

Outside the summer night was warm and the wind was coming down from the hills. I stood on the avenue with the lights of the bar behind me thinking of the Tour. In two days they would enter Belgium. Soon there would be the first time trial. The race was just beginning, and I could feel the building excitement as I walked home under the trees in the dark.

When I reached my apartment I undressed and lay on the top of the sheets listening to the sounds of the city through the open window. The wind was warm over my skin and I closed my eyes. Gradually my breathing slowed and my body relaxed. Then I heard Anne come in the door and drop her bags in the hall. She walked into the room and when

I opened my eyes and she was standing at the foot of the bed. Anne reached up and shook out her hair, and then slipped off her shoes, pulled her dress over her head, and lay down beside me on the bed. First there was the brush of her hair over my face, then her searching mouth and lips as we kissed, and I put my arms around her and rolled over feeling the warm length of her body beneath me. In the night her skin was pale against the sheets, her breasts were high and rounded, and her hair was long and dark and shining. She lay back and I moved over her, and there was the slow rising warmth and damp sweat, all of the smoothness and hollows, the soft flesh and rigid tenderness, the sudden parting warmth and tensed muscles, both of us moving together, and afterward the cool over our bodies as we lay on the bed listening to wind through the trees outside the window.

17

Two days later I walked up to the bar to watch the time trial. It was early evening and there was a light crowd. The bartender turned the television to the European sports channel. They were racing in the Belgian city of Huy, and I could see the boulevard along the Meuse with the barges moored on the banks, the houses across the river, and the water in the early morning sun. The boulevard was split by red-and-white barricades and lined with trees, and there were heavy crowds under the trees, and the Garde Republicaine in uniform keeping the crowd back. In the middle of the boulevard, facing the long straight, was the starting platform for the time trial.

In the time trials the riders started at two-minute intervals and raced alone against the clock. From Huy they rode into the country, through the rolling hills, and over the Côte de Pont de Bonne to the finish in Seraing thirty-five miles away. The fastest would cover the distance in a little over one hour. There were shorter time trials like the prologue, which lasted only lasted a few minutes, longer races like the GP des Nations, which was over three hours, uphill time trials, and team time trials like stage three from Mayenne to Alençon on the Fourth of July. The time trials always changed the overall, and while I never rode well in trials, I loved them because they were part of racing, and there was the pure clean feeling and distilled essence of riding alone as fast as you could on the road.

The time trial was the first real test of the Tour. One by one the announcer called the riders to the platform. Then the countdown began, and you could see them waiting at the top of the ramp, held upright on the bicycles, both feet clipped into the pedals, staring down the straight. In the background there was the beeping of the electronic timing device, the commisaire counted down with his fingers, five, four, three, two, gave the thumbs up on the one, moved his hand forward with a flat chopping motion on the zero, and the riders surged forward and rolled down the ramp to the cheers of the crowd. The motors pulled ahead, the team cars swung in behind, and they went down the boulevard along the Meuse.

They started in the reverse of the overall classification. The first to begin were the domestiques and team workers. Then there were the riders who hoped to place in the sprints, make the breaks, or finish high in the mountains. Finally, in the afternoon when the sun was high and the wind was blowing off the river swaying the trees along the boulevard, the leaders began racing.

Tony Rominger of Mapei-GB was the first leader with a chance of winning the Tour to start the time trial. They showed him at the top of the ramp, leaning forward over a black time trial bicycle, his face hidden behind a white helmet and mirrored visor. An older experienced Swiss, he had taken the Vuelta three times and placed second in the Tour in 1993. In the spring he had won the Tour of Romandie and the Giro. They gave him the count, and he rolled forward and came down the ramp onto the boulevard.

The second leader to start was Evgeni Berzin of Gewiss-Ballan. Berzin was Russian and had turned professional when the USSR collapsed. Young and blond with pale skin and a Northern European face, the year before he had taken Liège-Bastogne-Liège and the Giro. He was the first rider from the Eastern Bloc to win one of the great stage races, and the only rider to defeat Indurain for several years. Everybody said that one day he would win the Tour. In the spring he had taken the small Bicicleta Eibarresa in Spain, and five days before had led Gewiss-Ballan to first place in the team time trial in Alençon. Now, on the starting platform, he looked nervous, opening the collar of his jersey, flexing his hands on the brake levers, exhaling hard. When they gave him the count he sprinted down the ramp and quickly settled into pace.

Third was Alex Zülle of ONCE, a young Swiss, tall and handsome, with fine features, brown hair, and thick glasses that made him seem almost awkward. He had placed second in the Vuelta in 1993, had worn the yellow jersey in the Tour, and in the spring he had taken the Tour of Majorca, the Tour of Valencia, and the Pays du Basque, and placed second in the Tour of Switzerland. He was wearing a pink ONCE skinsuit and aerodynamic helmet, staring at the front wheel of his bicycle and bobbing his head with each count. On the zero he gritted his teeth, pushed down on the pedals, and rolled forward down the ramp.

Jalabert followed Zülle. After the crash at Le Havre, Jalabert had sprinted for all the time bonuses on stage five from Fecamp to Dunkirk, won by Blijlevens, stage six from Calais to Charleroi, won by Zabel, and stage seven to Liège, until he was just even on time with the yellow jersey on the road. In the Ardennes he had fallen back, but he was wearing the green jersey, and when he came down the ramp there was a slow building roar from the crowd, and you could see the French flags and Belgian flags and great banners swaying down the boulevard. The motors followed him along the Meuse, and then they switched back to the starting platform and I saw Indurain at top of the ramp.

There he is, I thought. Miguel Indurain. He had won the Tour four times in a row, and whenever I saw him there was the faint unreal quality and almost immortal presence of a great champion. They said that he was not as strong as past years, but in the spring he had taken the Midi Libre and Dauphine as always leading up to the Tour, and the day before in the Ardennes he had attacked on the Mont Theaux and gained one minute on all the others before the time trial even began. Now he was sitting over the bicycle with his head raised and his eyes shaded by the dark visor of his helmet looking down the straight. I heard the final electronic beeping of the timing device, the commisaire moved his hand forward in the flat chopping motion, and Indurain stood on the pedals and dropped down the ramp. There was the great roar of the crowd and the slow swaying waving motion on the sides, and Indurain went away down the boulevard.

The last rider to start was Johan Bruyneel of ONCE. In the Ardennes he had broken away with Indurain. Ahead of his leaders on the road, he could not share the work, drafted all the way to Liège, and came around at the line to win the stage and take the yellow jersey. Bruyneel was only thirty-one seconds ahead and nobody expected him to hold the jersey, but because he was the last rider the crowd cheered louder when he came down the ramp than for any other.

The motors picked them up in the country. They were leaned over the bicycles in the long time trialing positions, hands holding the forward pointing handlebars, backs flat and low, legs turning high gears, heads raised staring down the road. There were yellow fields and green rolling hills on the sides, and the crowds closed over the roads cheering and shouting and jumping back at the last moment as the riders passed. They came over the hills and down onto the wide highways, and you could see them surrounded by cars and motors on the long straights.

When they came through the first time check the splits showed and Rominger was fastest on the road. He was riding with his back hunched and his upper body rigid and his legs turning sharply, and he raced through the turns and down the narrow streets lined with flags. A few seconds later Berzin swept through the time check. He was a beautiful rider to watch, climbing out of the saddle, his young face flushed red, his hair blown back. Zülle came through one minute down, bent over the bicycle, his cheeks blowing as he breathed, his legs straining, his director shouting at him from the loudspeaker in the team car.

The motors dropped back and picked up Indurain. First I saw the white bicycle and white skinsuit and white helmet forming one continuous plane covered with red and yellow and blue Banesto colors, and then I saw Indurain sitting up in the saddle with his shoulders swaying back and forth, his arms tensing, and his great brown muscled legs turning over the pedals. His eyes were hidden behind the visor of his helmet, his chest was working as he breathed, and his skin was shining with sweat and water. He was riding a higher gear than all the others, and his legs were turning with molten grace and smooth fluid driving power. On the steepest climbs he moved his hands to the wide extensions, stood on the pedals, swung the bicycle back and forth, and surged forward with the disc wheels echoing on the ground. Indurain was the best time trial rider in the peloton and maybe the best the sport had ever seen, and he was wonderful to watch racing all the others and himself alone on the road. He passed Jalabert before the Côte de Pont de Bonne and came through the time check. When the splits showed there was one rider ahead by five seconds.

The window appeared with the number, 18, name, Riis, Bjarne, team, Gewiss-Ballan, and country, Denmark. The motors picked up Riis climbing through a narrow corridor of fans, his body swaying back and forth, his arms straining, his thin legs pushing down. I had not known Riis was such a good rider. He had placed fifth in the Tour in 1993 and was wearing the red jersey with the white cross of the Danish national champion, but nobody would have thought he could beat Indurain in a time trial. Riis did not have the smooth power of Indurain, but he had an intense, hard-driving form, and he was ahead by five seconds; he would have to hold on to Seraing.

In Seraing the road curved upward and narrowed into a chute that lead toward the finish. On the sides you could see the barricades, great crowds, and tents of the Village Arrivée. Along the straight were the red Coca-Cola, 2-Sport-3, and Fiat boards. Ahead was the gantry over the road and Festina clock counting down the time. The riders came into the chute and raced up the climb with the crowd leaning over the barricades cheering and waving flags and beating on the boards with their fists, and there was the slow terrible tension as they came down the straight with the previous fastest time displayed on the clock, the current time above, and the seconds running in positive or negative whether the rider was ahead or behind. Watching, I hoped that each rider would come faster, and also that the first time would stand and all the riders would finish well.

Rominger came up the climb and crossed the line at one hour, five minutes, fourteen seconds. It was the fastest time of the day. Berzin came up the climb with the clock showing 1:05:00 and the seconds running in the negative, and then the time passed and the seconds switched to the positive, and Berzin crossed the line at 1:05:54. Zülle came up the climb slowly with his body swaying, his shoulders rolling, and his face set in a grimace. He pushed over the last distance, dropped his head, reached for the strap of his helmet, and crossed the line at 1:08:44.

Riis came into the chute with another Gewiis-Ballan ahead and an ONCE behind. He sprinted up the climb along the barricades, his back bobbing, his legs straining over the gear, his mouth open like a scoop, with the clock showing 1:03:58 and the seconds running in the nega-tive. The crowd was chanting his name and waving the yellow flags and banners, and he came down the straight and crossed the line at 1:04:28. Riis swerved to a stop, slumped against the barricades, and collapsed in the road with his eyes closed and his chest heaving, and the news reporters and television crews closed over him.

The motors picked up Indurain on the road. He was climbing through a corridor of fans with the crowd cheering and motors forcing through honking their horns and the helicopter hovering over the trees. Then he came out on a wide highway, and behind you could see the white industrial buildings and low hills on the outskirts of Seraing. He was drawn forward on the bicycle, his mouth open breathing hard, his arms tensing with each stroke, his legs driving down with building power. You could see him feeling the approach of the finish, pushing himself harder, leaving everything on the road. There was nothing like Indurain in a time trial. At Luxembourg in 1992 he beat all the others by six minutes. He was the strongest rider in the peloton, and I knew that he would win the time trial.

Indurain swept into the chute with the red car and team car and motors spreading out behind in the bright haze on the road. He moved his hands to the extensions, stood on the pedals, and swung the bicycle back and forth, coming up the climb with his cheeks drawn back and his teeth flashing and his legs driving down. At the bottom of the screen they showed his number, 1, name, Indurain, Miguel, team, Banesto, country, Spain. On the clock was the current time, 1:03:50, and the previous time, 1:04:28, with the seconds running in the negative. He needs eleven seconds to take the jersey, I thought. Indurain sprinted down the straight with the crowd beating on the boards and chanting his name and shouting *allez, allez,* and the small yellow flags rippling on the sides and great Spanish banners waving overhead, and I found myself mouthing the seconds: fifteen, fourteen, thirteen. He crossed the line twelve seconds faster than Riis at 1:04:16 to take the yellow jersey.

Jalabert came down the straight over the line, Bruyneel finished, and the time trial was over. They showed the overall classification with

Indurain in yellow, Riis second at twenty three seconds, Berzin third at 2:20, Rominger fifth at 2:32, Jalabert sixth at 2:47, and Zülle farther down. That was the first important ranking of the top riders in the race. Early in the Tour you could not tell the winner, but usually you could tell who would not win, and when I saw the times there was the faint sad feeling knowing that for many riders the race was already over. On the podium Indurain pulled on the yellow jersey, smiling slightly, raising his arm, looking over the crowd in the Village Arrivée, and it was like all the other years that he won. The first week of the Tour was over. Now they would enter the mountains.

18

After the time trial there was a rest day and the Tour transferred to Geneva in the Swiss Alps. I went for a long ride, leaving late in the morning when the sun was high and the wind had dropped and the air was still and hot. As I climbed above the tunnel I knew that I was setting out for a long ride in the country. I would be on the road for most of the afternoon. More than one hundred miles. Five or six hours. I crested the climb, dropped on the short descent, and turned south into the park.

From the ridge I could see the white spread of Oakland and high buildings downtown shining in the sun. On the other side was the park and the burned brown country. When the road curved toward Oakland I turned onto the long descent and dropped into the canyon, gaining speed on the narrow road, racing through the shade, running out below. Then the road began to climb, and I stood on the pedals and slowed in the heat. That is what I loved about the summer: the feeling of working over the bicycle in the heat, your body slicked with sweat, the sun glaring bright, the country brown and dry. I sat down and rounded a corner onto a long straight with shimmering heat waves over the crest.

When I reached the top of the climb I could see the reservoir below surrounded by rolling hills and protected parkland. I went down the wide smooth grade into Castro Valley, rode through the town to the highway, and turned onto a smaller road that climbed into the rough wild ranchland above the Diablo Valley. The road was narrow and steep and shaded by heavy green trees, and over the crest there were open slopes and broken white rocks and high brown grass moving with the wind.

This must be what California looked like before the developments, I thought. The slopes spread down to the Diablo Valley, covered with a long cloud of hazy brown dust. Above the valley was Mount Diablo with the high peak against the clear blue sky. I went down into San Ramon and turned onto the boulevard that led past the mountain.

In the valley it was hot and I opened my jersey and rolled up my sleeves and shorts in the sun. The boulevard ran through Danville and I reached the long straight covered with an arched green canopy. I leaned down over the bicycle and settled into high gear.

Indurain had taken the time trial. Maybe he really would win the Tour. Nobody had ever won five Tours in a row, not even Merckx. Riis had come close in the time trial, though, closer than I or anybody else expected, and there were still Rominger and Berzin. Zülle was not finished either. We would see in the mountains. Now they would be at the hotels after going for a short ride to keep their legs fresh, they would have had their massages and their afternoon naps, and they would be resting and waiting and thinking about the mountains, knowing how hard the climbs would be, hoping to survive, wishing the high passes were behind them. The mountains began with two days in the Alps.

I passed Mount Diablo and turned onto the smaller roads that led back toward Moraga. My skin was dry and there was a heavy deadened fatigue in my legs. Sitting up on the bicycle I drank the rest of my water, and then stood on the pedals to stretch my muscles, and rode slowly back toward the hills. Fifteen miles from home. One more hour.

Some days in the summer the mist came off the ocean and covered the country. When I rode into Moraga it was still sunny and bright, but above I could see the mist moving over the ridge. I rode through the town, crested the short steep hill, and dropped into the canyon. As I began to climb the sun faded and the air grew damp and cold and the mist closed over the road. Then I could not see the country and there was only the road leading upward into the heavy white mist. I shifted gears to stay warm and climbed higher.

19

The mountain stages of the Tour were shown late at night because they were so long. When I came up to the bar it was crowded, the lights were turned low, and music was playing. I sat down at the counter and the bartender switched on the television. I was the only person in the bar watching the Tour. The others were ordering drinks and gathering for the evening. I sat alone staring at the silent screen. There was the peloton leaving Le Grand Bornand. It was bright and sunny, the crowds were cheering, and the people on the balconies of the old buildings were waving handkerchiefs as the caravan passed. They went out of the town riding down a long narrow valley with alpine wood-and-stucco chalets, smooth green pastures, and dark green forests. At the head of the valley were the towering gray rock faces and snow-covered peaks of the Savoie Alps.

It was the mountains that made the great tours. I had never seen the Tour de France, but I had watched the 1993 Giro d'Italia from the roadside in the Dolomites. That was the first time I saw the professionals. The peloton rode from Dozza to Asiago. Early in the morning I left the hotel where I was staying with my club and we rode our bicycles up the last climb of the race. Already there were heavy crowds on the mountain and many people who camped the night before or drove up in the dark. They had painted the names of the riders on the road and placed banners and flags on the sides, and as we climbed they cheered as if we were part of the Giro.

We stopped at a switchback above the town of Conco where we could watch the riders come up the valley, through the town, and around the switchback. Below the mountain sloped down to the foothills and the flat plain covered with small squares of fields and towns all the way to Venice. Above were the high pine forests and open pastures of the Altopiano and the peaks of Mount Erio and Mount Fior.

The first sign of the race were the policemen, or carabinieri, on motorcycles clearing the road. Then the great publicity caravan passed like a circus, winding slowly up the valley, through Conco, and around the switchback. There was a great bus shaped like a molded shoe, a car with an arm and wristwatch, a rolling piece of cheese, a cylindrical bottle of mineral water on wheels. These were the sponsors of the race, and as they passed you could hear the loudspeakers blaring advertisements over the cheers of the crowd, and the road was showered with product samples, promotional brochures, and pink paper hats and jerseys.

Following the publicity caravan were more motors and several advance cars, and we all crossed to the far side of the road, looking down the valley as the race approached. Then, far below, the helicopter appeared, tracking along the side of the mountain with its shadow flying over the forest. The helicopter slowly rose in the valley, the distant whup-whup-whup becoming louder, and suddenly there were shouts—*due, due*—as two riders came out from beneath the trees moving slowly toward Conco.

More carabinieri passed, faster and with greater urgency, honking their horns and swerving to keep the crowd back, several advance cars, and a commisaire car. Then there was the red car driving fast with the tires squealing and the director standing out of the roof with his hands braced looking back down the road, the helicopter was hovering overhead with the loud beating whine and the dust swirling in the wind, a service motor passed with the passenger crouched forward, and then, traveling much faster than seemed possible, two riders came up from below, around the switchback, and past in the road, the roar of the crowd following them up the climb.

It was Claudio Chiappucci on the attack, standing on the pedals and sweeping around the steep inside of the switchback, sprinting up the straight, his jet black hair streaming back from his tan, flat-nosed, native American Indian-looking face, his eyes wide and excited. That was the way I liked to remember him, always attacking in the mountains. Behind Chiappucci was Des Las Quevas, covering the break for Banesto.

The peloton came up from below and around the switchback. Mercatone-Uno was working on the front for Lealli in the *maglia rosa*. Behind was Indurain, taller than I imagined, sitting straight on the bicycle with his hands resting on the tops of the bars and his legs turning smoothly. He was wearing a clean white jersey, his face was calm and composed, and his eyes were hidden behind dark sunglasses. In the middle of the peloton I could see Bugno wearing the world champion jersey, face pale and tired, eyes red-rimmed, and at the back of the line was LeMond, leaning low over the handlebars with a strained hollow expression. A few days later Indurain took the *maglia rosa* and went on to win the Giro. The following year Chiappucci and Bugno abandoned the Tour, and soon afterward LeMond retired. The rest of the peloton passed with a collective rush, the bright colors of the jerseys and the bicycles flashing in the sun, and the crowd closed over the road.

Behind was the long line of follow cars, the line of press cars and commisaire cars, and the great team buses that swung around the switchbacks with the crowd spilling out of the way cheering for each team. Mixed in with the caravan were the riders who had been dropped, drafting the cars and moving up on the sides. The crowd ran alongside, cheering and pouring water over their backs, and pushing those who were struggling around the switchback and up the straights. Finally there were the last riders, and the stray cars and motors. As suddenly they had come, the helicopter, honking horns, and cheers were gone, and we were left by the switchback with the sounds receding up the climb, and the pink papers blowing away over the slopes. We started down past the long line of cars and streams of people walking in the road. That was how the great Tours passed in the mountains.

In the bar I watched the peloton come over the Col de Marais, the Col de L'Epine, and the Col de Hery. When they reached the Col des Saisies there was already a small front group, and they rode up through a forest and rounded a switchback. Then Zülle attacked. He sprinted up the climb and moved clear with a TVM rider and Federico Muñoz of Kelme, and the motors picked them up near the summit with Zülle leading. The Col des Saisies was not one of the higher mountains, and there were still pines over the slopes and burned yellow grass and open meadows hazy in the heat. Muñoz sprinted under the red Champion banner taking the mountain points over the summit, and they began the long descent into the valley.

Zülle led on the descent, the TVM rider close on his wheel, the little climber from Kelme several lengths back. On the steep roads they pulled ahead of the motors, and you could see them sit up and slow around the switchbacks, and then stand on the pedals and sprint back to speed on the straights. Slowly the country spread out on the sides, the road leveled, and you could see the valley below with the small squares of the fields, the white of the towns, and the dark green hanging masses of the higher mountains

The peloton came over the summit of the Col de Saisies, one minute and forty seconds behind the break. Banesto was working on the front and when they came down into the valley you could see Indurain in the yellow jersey, surrounded by his high mountain domestiques. Now we will see Banesto on the front always, I thought. They will set the pace on the climbs, lead down the descents, and pull through the valleys, keeping Indurain in yellow. The break was crossing the valley. Zülle was leading and he looked strong with body low on the bicycle, his arms and legs working rhythmically, his head raised in the wind. The ONCE team car came up and the director Manolo Saiz gave him the time gap and handed up a bottle of water; Zülle took the bottle, drank, and settled back into the steady pace. Every so often the TVM rider or Muñoz pulled through, and they came down the straight roads past rows of trees and yellow fields and small farmhouses, riding toward the Cormet de Roseland, towering over the valley, the summit lost in clouds.

Lance Armstrong was chasing the break across the valley. They showed him driving forward with his aggressive muscular style on the bicycle. He always looked like he was attacking when he rode. Armstrong won everything in America and then went to Europe and won Worlds. He was so strong that nobody knew, really, what he could do in the sport. Greg LeMond was still the only American to take the Tour. He had won in 1986 from Hinault, in 1989 from Fignon, and for the last time in 1990. That was when we had the 7-Eleven team and Davis Phinney and Andy Hampsten. Hampsten was still famous in Italy for climbing the Gavia pass in the middle of a snow storm to take the *maglia rosa*. Now LeMond and Phinney and Hampsten had retired, 7-Eleven had become Motorola, and we had Armstrong and Frankie Andreu, who had ridden three Tours as a domestique. While it was nice to see an American world champion and a good solid American domestique working in Europe, it would have been wonderful to see an American take the Tour on an American team. That was hard to imagine, but watching Armstrong chase across the valley, I thought that one day it might be possible.

The break was onto the Cormet de Roseland. They were climbing up through the forest on the lower slopes, and Zülle was forcing the pace. The motor drew alongside and showed him leaning forward over the handlebars and driving down on the pedals, and they came up through the forest under the light green trees with the sun bright and hot on the road. Slowly Muñoz fell behind, the TVM rider dropped back, and Zülle was alone.

Zülle had not had a good ride in the time trial, but he attacked on the first mountain, used the others through the valley, and moved clear on the second to last climb. Now he was standing on the pedals and swinging the bicycle back and forth, his jersey open, his body covered with a sheen of sweat, looking up toward the summit. Zülle came out of the trees, and in the distance to the south you could see Mont Blanc and the Chamoix Valley and the Aiguilles du Midi. Below was the small valley with the surrounding dark green mountains, and the thin white line of the peloton coming onto the Roseland. The gap showed at two minutes. If he held on over the summit and through the valley he could win the stage. If the gap opened he could take the yellow jersey. As he climbed the country fell away, there was the growing feeling of height and openness, and he came out on the high smooth green slopes. Above the sky was clear and blue, and you could see the road leading up into the bottom of the heavy gray clouds. Another climb. Another hour of solitary grinding exertion. Another summit before the respite of the descent.

The second motor picked up the peloton on the lower slopes of the Roseland. They were coming up through the forest and the high mountain domestiques were working on the front. Gerard Rué was the head domestique for Banesto; you always saw him setting the pace on the climbs, jaw thrust forward, teeth gritted, sandy red hair blown back. They caught Armstrong, Muñoz, and the TVM rider, and the motor dropped back showing the others in the small group. At the back of the line was Berzin, leaning low over the handlebars, his head down, his shoulders swaying back and forth. The others pulled away and receded up the road. The motors followed for a while showing Berzin climbing alone, and then one of the Gewiss-Ballan domestiques dropped back to set the pace, and the two disappeared in the caravan.

High on the mountain the ONCE team car pulled alongside Zülle, and Saiz shouted the time check over the sound of the car. He had 3:30. Zülle came into the clouds on the Roseland, and suddenly the sky was dark and white mist closed over the road, with water beading on the lens of the cameras and the lights of the follow cars shining yellow behind. In the mountains the riders traversed great distances from the summits to the valleys, and often the changes in weather were extreme. Zülle was climbing out of the saddle, the bicycle surging forward, his body swaying sinuously, his face pale and wet and cold. Then, in the mist, there were camping vans and cars along the road, people cheering and running alongside, and great crowds around the switchbacks. He must be nearing the summit, I thought. The mist lifted and you could see the green slopes scattered with rocks, the black rock faces streaked with snow, and the red-and-white Champion banner over the summit. Zülle rode under the banner and the gap came up at 5:00 with the words, Maillot Jaune. Zülle was the new yellow jersey on the road. He still had the long descent and run through the valley and final climb to La Plagne, and he came over the summit without slowing, spit to clear his mouth, and began the long descent.

On the descent there were no cars and no crowds and only the empty country. The road was narrow and steep, the surface was wet and rough, and on the sides great ravines dropped away into the clouds. Zülle tucked low over the bicycle, the wind blowing his hair back and fluttering the sleeves of his jersey, and you could see him grimacing through the spray from the wheels and flexing his hands on the brake levers to keep his fingers from cramping in the cold. He pulled ahead of the motors and disappeared into the mist, the sound of his brakes fading around the corners. Don't crash now, I thought, not when you're leading the Tour. I remembered when Zülle crashed out of the lead of the Vuelta on a cold wet stage in the mountains. The motors picked up Zülle lower on the mountain, coming down out of the clouds toward the Aime Valley. The sun was shining, the sky was clear and blue, and below you could see the squares of the fields and the small town of Bourg St. Maurice. Across the valley was the final climb to La Plagne.

The peloton came over the summit of the Roseland and the riders sat up and took the newspapers offered by the fans, stuffed the papers under their jerseys to block the wind, and dropped into the mist. The motors picked them up lower on the mountain, and they rode down through Bourg St. Maurice and reached the Aime Valley.

Zülle was onto La Plagne. They showed him coming up through the forest with the heavy crowd and motors following and helicopter beating above. The gap had grown to 5:10. He was still the yellow jersey on the road. Now he must be thinking of the Tour, I said to myself. Now on the final climb ahead of the others he must be thinking of winning the Tour.

The helicopter showed the peloton crossing the valley. When they reached La Plagne the motors picked them up coming through the forest under the heavy green trees with the sun bright and hot and the crowd cheering. The group had grown smaller. Bugno had been dropped and Berzin was being paced through Aime Valley by his teammates. Rué took them up the lower slopes, and then he pulled to the side and dropped back, and Aparicio came through on the front. Aparicio was the last Banesto high mountain domestique. He held the pace for as long as he could, and then sat up and slowed, Tonkov of

Lampre attacked, and the others passed on both sides.

When they came out from the forest Indurain was riding on the front. He looked back over his shoulder. Behind were Riis and Ivan Gotti of Gewiss-Ballan, Rominger and Laurent Escartin of Mapei-GB, Jalabert and Mauri of ONCE, Virenque and Dufaux of Festina, Pantani and Chiappucci of Carrera, Laudelino Cubino and Muñoz of Kelme, Alvaro Mejia of Motorola, Oscar Pellicioli of Polti, Emmanuel Magnien of Castorama, and the young rider Paulo Lanfranchi of Brecialat. Indurain was alone. All of his domestiques had been dropped, and he was surrounded by climbers. Now they would attack.

Indurain turned around and looked back up the road. He leaned forward and shifted into a higher gear, and gradually began pedaling faster. Then he moved his hands to the drops, and you could see his arms pulling and his shoulders swaying and his legs driving down. Suddenly the group was stretched into line. Indurain did not stand on the pedals or sprint or attack: He smoothly increased the pace, and behind, one by one, the others fell behind.

Jalabert swung off and dropped back. Rominger sat up and slowed. Riis moved to the side and disappeared. Cubino jumped hard and sprinted up to Indurain, holding his wheel for a few strokes, and then faded, standing on pedals and weaving back and forth in the road. Gotti passed Cubino and reached Indurain, they swept around a corner, Indurain looked over his shoulder and increased the pace, and Gotti dropped back. Indurain was riding them all off his wheel. After the whole year of training, the slow build-up to the Tour, and the first week of waiting and wondering, it was clear. They could not attack. He was too strong. Lanfranchi, the last rider, came around Gotti and sprinted up to Indurain. They rounded a switchback, with the 2-Sport-3 banner on the inside, and then Lanfranchi sat down and fell back, and Indurain was alone. He went up through the small alpine town of Macot with the church bells ringing in the background, caught and passed Tonkov, and came above into the high alpine country. The slopes fell away toward the valley below, and you could see the road winding down the mountain, and the peloton broken into small groups and single riders moving slowly up the climb. Ahead were the smooth green pastures and clear blue sky and summit covered with clouds.

His full name was Miguel Angel Indurain-Larraya. He had grown up in the town of Villava in the Navarra province of the Basque territory of Spain. His family farmed in the foothills of the Pyrénées. When he was eleven years old he began racing for his hometown team, Villava VC Navarra. Slowly he moved up through the categories, and eventually rode the Olympics for Spain. In 1984 he turned professional for Reynolds, and began working as a domestique for the Spanish champion Pedro Delgado.

If you looked at his *palmares* you saw that he had won many of the smaller stage races in Spain and France: the Tour of Murcia, the Tour of Galacia, the Tour of Catalonia, the Tour of Burgos, and the Tour de l'Avenir. Then in 1989 he had won Paris-Nice and Criterium International. I remembered the pictures of Indurain wearing the white jersey in Nice; his body was heavier, his skin pale, but he had the same handsome Basque face, dark serious eyes, and calm inward expression. Nobody knew him then, but that summer in the Pyrénées he won his first stage of the Tour.

Now they showed him climbing toward La Plagne, six years later, after he had won the Tour four times and the Giro twice, and set the hour record at Bordeaux. His face looked older, his body was lean and hard, and his eyes were shaded behind dark sunglasses. He had become the great champion of the decade. He was not like Hinault, driven by fierce pride and iron independence, whom all the other riders feared; nor Merckx, the greatest rider in the history of the sport, who won everything from the smallest kermesse to the Tour de France for over five hundred victories as a professional; nor Anquetil, a gentleman whose life was like a movie; nor Coppi, a tragic hero who inspired his country with such passion that two-hundred thousand people attended his funeral. Indurain was still the same simple modest rider from Navarra. Some people said that he was not exciting to watch, that he founded each Tour victory on the time trials, that he never attacked in the mountains, and that he did not show the emotions of a true champion. While it was true that he always took the first long time trial and then defended his lead overall, there was no racing I knew more exciting than the two stages he had won in the mountains, the stage to Val Louron in 1991 when he attacked over the Tourmalet, or the stage to Hautacam in 1994 where he came up the mountain through heavy mist to win the Tour. He expressed himself on the bicycle the way that he was most suited, gave everything he had in the areas where he was strongest, and then rode with control and dignity and restraint. In bicycle racing there were many ways to win, and often it was not the strongest rider who crossed the line first, but the smartest, luckiest, or the rider with the best team. Indurain always won without surprise or trickery or tactics. He won with pure strength against the others at the times when it mattered most. And he never took more than he needed to win the Tour, leaving the stages and the smaller races for the other riders. He was the most respectful and respected champion in modern cycling. As he climbed toward La Plagne, leaning forward over the bicycle, his legs driving round, his eyes looking up toward the summit, the time gap to Zülle slowly began to fall: 4:30, 4:00, 3:30.

The motors picked up Zülle racing into the clouds. The sky was dark, the lights of the follow cars were shining through the mist, and the crowd was lining the road cheering and shouting and running alongside. Zülle swept around a switchback and came up the straight, standing on the pedals and swinging the bicycle back and forth, his shoulders swaying, his cheeks sucking and blowing as he breathed, his face shining with sweat. He must know Indurain is coming, I thought. He would have the time checks, but he would not know that Indurain is coming alone, leaned over the handlebars, driving up the mountain, on-coming, up-coming, racing into the clouds. The gap showed at 3:00. With each kilometer Indurain was drawing closer.

Zülle was nearing the summit. The crowd was larger and they closed over the road forming a narrow corridor. There was no other sport that I knew where the fans got so close. They gave the riders water in the heat and newspapers in the cold, pushed those who were struggling, and ran alongside the champions, touching them as they passed. They were part of the race. Zülle came up the corridor, swept around a switchback, and broke onto the summit plateau. The road flattened, and behind you could see the smooth green slopes, broken gray boulders, and the steep gray face of the summit.

Zülle sat up on the bicycle and closed his jersey, and then shifted gears and sprinted past the brown wooden chalets and white apartment blocks of the ski station. The road widened and the crowd was kept back by barricades, and he raced over the plateau with his jersey and hair blown flat in the wind. He swept into the curving chute and turned onto the straight, and the motors and the red car with flashing lights spread out behind. He had stayed away over three mountains, had been the yellow jersey on the road, and was going to win the stage. The crowd cheered, and Zülle came down the straight keeping close to the barricades with the banners and flags waving on the sides. Finally he sat up on the bicycle, his face broke into a smile, and he crossed himself, stretched his arms overhead in a salute, and coasted over the line.

The second motor picked up Indurain racing through the clouds toward the summit. He was banking into the corners and overtaking the motors, his body working, his face shining with sweat, his lips drawn back showing his teeth. As he came up the corridor the fans chanted his name, In-du-rain, In-du-rain, with the great red-yellow-red Spanish flags waving overhead. Then he broke onto the wide summit plateau where the road flattened. The gap showed at 2:30. Indurain was no longer chasing Zülle, he was racing to gain time on the others, open the gaps, and extend his lead in the Tour. He passed the chalets and apartment blocks and came onto the wide open road where the crowd was kept back by the barricades, and then he turned onto the curving straight with the motors and follow cars spreading out behind. When Indurain came into sight the crowd roared, and he sprinted down the straight along the barricades with his head tilted to the side, his teeth gritted, and the yellow jersey flat in the wind. Finally he sat down, pushed over the last distance, and lunged forward over the line, two minutes and two seconds behind Zülle.

They showed the rest of the peloton coming up through the clouds to La Plagne. Tonkov was climbing alone, Pantani and Gotti were riding together, Rominger, Virenque, Chiappucci, and Lanfranchi had formed a small group. Tonkov finished at 4:11, Pantani and Gotti at 4:37, the Rominger group at 6:05. Riis, Jalabert, and Berzin were farther back. It began to rain lightly and still riders were finishing in small groups or alone, coming down the straight with the lights of the follow cars shining behind and the crowd cheering.

Slowly the clouds cleared and the rain stopped and you could see the smooth green plateau in the bright sun, the shadows of the clouds moving over, and the tall white towers of the ski resort. On the television they showed the overall classification. Indurain kept the yellow jersey, Zülle was second at 2:27, Riis third at 5:58, Rominger fourth at 6:35, Gotti fifth at 6:54. The first mountain stage was over. Zülle had moved into the top three, and Jalabert and Berzin had fallen back. Some riders were already over an hour behind. In the background the plateau dropped away to a wide green valley. Behind were the peaks of the Courchevel and the Val d'Isere and the Iseran, surrounded by the high gray and white Alps.

20

The day after the first mountain stage we raced a criterium in the valley south of San Jose. That morning was cold and gray and overcast, and the wind was coming off the ocean. We drove down through Oakland to San Jose, continued south, and came out in a narrow valley surrounded by flat bare fields and low brown mountains. The clouds slowly moved away, the sun began to shine, and when we reached the race it was bright and clear and the wind was still blowing hard. The course went around a field on the outskirts of the developments. Each lap was one mile long. There was a windbreak of trees along the backstretch, a line of houses behind, and in the distance the burned brown hills and wide blue sky. At the smaller summer races there was no stage for the officials, no announcer, and no music, and the race did not have the festive feeling of the criteriums in the spring.

We staged on the road under the banner and there were a few cheers as we rolled away from the line and turned the first corner into the wind. When the crosswind came up the front spread into an echelon, and the rest of the pack flattened in line against the side of the road. I leaned down over the bicycle, fighting to hold the handlebars straight in the wind, and looked up the line; the echelon was stretched across the road with the riders crouched over the bicycles racing hard, their legs moving in unison, the colors of the jerseys bright in the sun. I knew that I had to move to the front. The echelon would pull away, everybody else would be dropped, and if I did not make it now I would never finish with the pack. I swung out of the draft and sprinted up the line.

When I reached the echelon I drew onto the last wheel, riding behind outside the rotation. I was breathing hard and my legs were already tired and I knew that I could not ride much longer in the wind. Leaning with my shoulder I pushed into the echelon. It was very tight, with my handlebars brushing the rider beside me and my tires running in the dirt on the edge of the road, but it was faster out of the wind, and slowly I felt my body recover. I had made the echelon. Turning my head I looked back down the road and saw the pack stretched into a long line with the fields and bare brown mountains in the background. When the professionals formed an echelon there was always a second echelon behind, and sometimes a third and fourth, the whole peloton running in diagonal lines across the road, especially in Holland and Belgium where there were always crosswinds over the flats. It was the only way to ride into the wind, but I knew that behind they would not form a second echelon, they would not work together, and they would chase alone until they were dropped.

We came down the straight and turned the corner into the headwind and the echelon swung into a paceline. I went up through the rotation and took my pull, and we turned onto the backstretch under the trees. In the shelter I drank quickly, stood on the pedals to stretch my legs, and sat back down. The front had not slowed. They were already moving to the outside for the final corner, and we banked over the road and came upright on the straight. The wind was blowing from behind and I drew myself forward on the saddle, shifted up through the gears, and swept past the finish in the smooth silent rush of the tailwind.

At the front we worked together in steady rotation, forming echelons in the crosswind and pacelines on the straights, slowing only on the backstretch under the trees, and gradually we pulled ahead of the others. Looking back across the fields you could see the riders chasing alone. Finally we came around the course and the officials pulled the last riders and the road was clear.

When all the others had been pulled the pack slowed. I sat up from the drops with my hands numb from holding the bars and my legs deadened and weak. The wind was moving the grass in waves over the fields, and you could see the dust rising and the sky cleared of clouds. We were coming around for the last lap and I knew the sprint would be long and drawn out with the tailwind. I just hope nobody attacks, I thought. If they attack and we chase I don't know if I can hold on. We turned the final corner and came down the straight, sweeping past the finish with the cheers of the crowd and the ringing bell carried away by the wind.

In the crosswind the front slowed and the sides massed forward and the pack spread out on the road. Nobody wanted to lead on the last lap. I stood on the pedals and moved up a few positions, and then a rider attacked from behind and the pack began to chase, and there was no echelon anymore, and only the long single line fighting into the crosswind. I leaned over the bicycle and pushed forward into the wind with heavy surging strokes, holding the wheel ahead, and we turned the corner into the headwind. The wind whipped the pack into line, and there was the long slow push down the straight with the distance slowly closing to the shelter of the trees on the backstretch.

Finally we turned out of the wind and the pack picked up speed and a rider attacked from behind. I heard him coming past and jumped hard and caught his wheel, and we sprinted away down the road. Letting the bicycle come forward beneath me I sat down and looked back over my shoulder. We had a small gap and the pack was stretched in line with the rider on the front chasing hard. The final corner was coming up fast. We moved to the outside, banked into the corner, and rounded onto the straight. The first rider swung wide, and I came through on the front.

I felt the wind take me from behind and I pulled myself forward and shifted into the last gear. Far down the straight I could see the banner blown taut like a sail and the small crowd cheering silently. Ducking my head I looked back under my arm. The pack was sweeping around the corner. They were too close. If only he took you a little farther, I thought. Why did he attack if he was going to pull off? There is nothing you can do now. Just put your head down and sprint. Then I was out of the saddle, and I moved to the center of the road and began sprinting.

The gear quickly came over and my legs spun out and I sat down and narrowed my body in the wind. The banner was drawing closer and the sides were still clear and in the silent rushing I could hear my forced breaths and the faint cheers of the crowd. Suddenly the pack came over with the riders sprinting on both sides and the bicycles flashing back and forth and the front driving forward, and I sat up and watched them spread out on the straight. It was over. They crossed the line and I coasted under the banner in the middle of the pack.

21

O n the second day in the mountains the Tour began in the town of Aime at the base of La Plagne. I came up to the bar and the bartender turned on the television. They were climbing the Col de la Madeleine. The peloton was all together riding slowly, and you could see the line across the front and the long caravan stretched down the mountain. The Tour had not been up the Madeleine for years. It was a two thousand meter summit, and as they climbed the trees gradually fell away, the slopes spread out smooth and green, there were the broken rocks, fields of snow, and finally the great towering snow-covered Lauziere peak, with the Col de la Croix de Fer and L'Alpe d'Huez in the distance to the south, where they would finish at the end of the day.

Virenque took the mountain points under the banner, and they crested the summit and began the long descent into the Maurienne Valley. The valley was covered with white mist like a cloud, and the peaks of the surrounding mountains were rising into the sun. The helicopter flew straight out from the summit to pick them up below.

They crossed the valley and came through the small town of St. John de Maurienne, and at the base of the Col de la Croix de Fer, Dufaux attacked. One by one others bridged, and soon there were nine riders in the break. The first motor showed them climbing in line: Dufaux, Virenque, Jalabert, Bruyneel, Gotti, Escartin, Muñoz, Elli of

MG-Technogym, and an AKI rider I did not recognize. Üdo Bolts bridged across, then Mejia, and there were eleven. The gap showed at nine minutes. It was a large break, and I was surprised to see them move clear so early in the stage. Finally Aparicio came up, marking the break for Banesto, and they went up the climb toward the summit.

Rué led the peloton onto the Croix de Fer. Rominger had fallen back, and Berzin had been dropped on the Madeleine. The motors picked up Berzin in the Maurienne Valley. He had sent his domestiques on ahead and he was riding alone, his jersey open in the heat, his blond hair streaked dark with sweat, his legs turning slowly. The Gewiss-Ballan car came up and you saw him talking to the director through the window, and at the feed zone in Maurelon Berzin pulled to a stop, climbed off his bicycle, and walked to the team car. He was finished. They would wait for the caravan to pass and drive on to the finish. The motors waited beside the car, and you could see the cameramen fighting for position to shoot Berzin. Then the car pulled away and disappeared, and the small window came up with the word, *Abandonner,* and the long list of riders who had left the race that day: Berzin, Mario Chiesa, Cipollini, Durand, Maurizio Fondriest, Olaf Ludwig, Vanderaerden.

Sometimes it was hard to watch in the mountains. Many of the riders were weak or sick or injured, and they fell behind on the climbs and dropped back through the caravan until they were alone. They forced themselves to continue, far behind the peloton, riding slower and slower, standing on the pedals and leaning all their weight on each stroke, weaving back and forth on the road, sitting down and pushing, their faces strained and desperate. Finally they climbed off their bicycles and stopped racing. Sometimes you saw them crying by the side of the road, not wanting to abandon, knowing they had to abandon, surrounded by the television crews and the photographers and crowd. Often they continued until they were forced to stop. There was a time limit for each stage. If riders finished outside the time limit they were cut from the race. The commisaires would strip the numbers from their jerseys, take their bicycles, and the riders would climb into the back of the broom wagon. Every day they made a show of one rider or another abandoning the Tour. It was brutal, but in the mountains there were also the long epic breaks, the riders dropping on the descents, crossing the valleys, and climbing toward the summits, and it was beautiful.

Sitting at the crowded bar, watching riders abandon the Tour, I felt separated from the people around me. You had to race to know what it was like push yourself so hard that it was only the bicycle holding you upright, to drive yourself to your limits, to have a desire for something so strong that nothing else mattered. I was tired from the races, and with the fatigue was a faint fear, not yet fully formed in my mind, as if invisible around the corners of a long climb, that I was running out of time. It was the middle of the summer. I needed to find the form that I had in the spring. I needed to place. I needed to upgrade to Pro/I-II.

Virenque lead the break on the Croix de Fer, climbing out of the saddle with his thin body swaying back and forth, his arms and legs working hard, his young face excited. In 1994 he had taken the stage to Luz Ardiden, and he was one of the best climbers in the peloton. The French loved him, and as he passed they cheered and shouted and ran alongside waving flags. Behind the mountain dropped away steeply, and you could see the green ridges, runs of bare dirt, wide valley, and across the valley the snow-covered peaks and thin white clouds at the same level. Higher the road narrowed and there were steep walls and great massed yellow rocks near the summit. Over the rocks and in lines along the road was a great crowd, the bright colors and banners and flags moving in the sun, and the break came up through the narrow cleft in the rocks and over the summit. Virenque took the mountain points, the AKI rider and Aparicio dropped back, and the break began the long descent into the Romanche Valley.

The peloton came over the summit of the Croix de Fer one minute and thirty seconds behind the break, with Rué leading the small front group. The motors lost them on the descent, and when they picked them up in the Romanche Valley Aparicio had been caught and was working with Carrera. They were in the middle of the Alps. Behind were the Croix de Fer and the Glandon, to the west Grenoble, to the southeast toward Briançon the Lauterets, the Galibier, and Serre Chevalier, and across the border in Italy the long climb to Sestriere. Ahead was the small town of Bourg d'Oisans and L'Alpe d'Huez.

The break came through Bourg d'Oisans and took the left hand turn onto L'Alpe d'Huez. Immediately the road was steep and they slowed and began to climb. They rounded the first and second switchbacks, called lacets, the snow-covered Massif des Escrins in the background, the thin line of the peloton threading through the town below. The road led up through the forest and came out above, and there were the nineteen additional lacets tracking up the mountain toward the summit.

They had reached L'Alpe d'Huez. It was not as high as the Iseran nor the Tourmalet, as barren as the Izoard nor the bare white Ventoux, as steep as the Stelvio nor the Mortirolo, but it was the most famous mountain in cycling, and the most prestigious stage for climbers. They first raced up L'Alpe d'Huez in 1952. Since then the yellow jersey had changed seven times on the climb, eleven times the yellow jersey at the summit went on to win the Tour, and once half the peloton had finished outside the time limit, and the commisaires had to grant a reprieve so that the race could continue. In the winter the ski station at the summit was crowded with people on holiday. In the summer the mountain was empty and there were cable cars for skiing on the high glacier. Then, in July, more than 150,000 fans came to L'Alpe d'Huez to watch the Tour.

The break was coming up through the heavy forest and bright sun and cheering crowd. Dufaux and Bruyneel were working on the front. They swung round a lacet and Roberto Elli attacked, moving clear and sitting down and pushing forward on the steep road. The gap came up at eleven seconds. They showed the others chasing hard, and the break began come apart. Muñoz slowly dropped back, Mejia fell behind, and then Bruyneel and Bolts. Finally Gotti attacked and went away up the road, leaving Virenque, Jalabert, Escartin, and Dufaux in a small group.

Banesto and Carrera led the peloton through Bourg d'Oisans and onto L'Alpe d'Huez. The motors showed them from the front, and a Carrera rider moved up the outside and attacked. He sprinted away, another rider bridged, and when they came closer I saw that it was Pantani and Laurent Maduas.

Marco Pantani was one of the best climbers in the peloton. The year before he had taken the Merano and Aprica stages of the Giro, and placed third in the Tour. They said that he would never win the overall because he could not time trial, but he could certainly climb. He was standing on the pedals and swinging the handlebars from side to side, his little body moving over the bicycle, his bald head gleaming with sweat, his brow furrowed from the effort. Pantani sat down and shifted gears, and then stood on the pedals and accelerated, and Maduas fell behind. He caught Muñoz, Mejia, Elli, Bruyneel, and Bolts, and you could see the remains of the break moving up through the crowd. Pantani reached the break and went straight past on the opposite side of the road. He caught Gotti, crossed to the outside, looked back over his shoulder, and slowly Gotti dropped back, and Pantani was alone.

He climbs like the greats, I thought, Bobet or Jiminez or Bahomantes. Now most riders climbed with the high steady pace of the modern style, but Pantani had the classic style of the small light rider, dancing on the pedals, darting ahead, flying up the mountains. Virenque might have been wearing the red-and-white jersey, but Pantani was the better climber. Pantani came up through the crowd, swept around a lacet, and sprinted up the straight with the motors leading and the yellow service car following behind. The gap showed at fifty seconds. He was racing for L'Alpe d'Huez.

The peloton was climbing through the forest. Rué was setting the pace and the group had grown smaller. Behind were Indurain, Zülle, Riis, Chiappucci, Tonkov, and Rominger, who had fought back through the valley. As they swung around a lacet, Riis stood on the pedals and attacked, and Rué did not change the rhythm of his pedaling. Then Zülle jumped away and moved clear, sitting down and driving forward, and still Rué did not respond. The race was breaking apart. The riders in second, third, fifth, and sixth places overall were ahead on the road, and Indurain was not reacting. They were attacking, and I felt a hollow chilled fear as I watched.

Finally Rué began to slow. His arms were pulling weakly, his legs were straining, and he moved to the side and dropped back. Indurain came through on the front. Again he did not stand on the pedals or sprint or attack. Again he leaned forward and shifted into a high gear. Again the group was suddenly stretched into line. Indurain quickly brought Zülle back, went straight past, and the two pulled away from the others.

Ahead on the road a small chase group had formed behind Pantani. The motors showed them climbing in a line, and at the bottom of the television screen the small window came up with the word, *Poursuivants*, and the names, Riis, Jalabert, Virenque, Gotti, Escartin, Dufaux, Maduas. The leaders had all changed: Berzin had dropped back and Riis was leading Gewiss-Ballan; Rominger had fallen behind and Escartin was leading Mapei-GB; Durand had abandoned and Maduas was leading Castorama.

Indurain and Zülle reached the chase group, swung round a lacet with the white writing and the cheering crowd, and passed on the outside of the road. As they passed Riis jumped onto the last wheel and the three riders went up the mountain. Indurain would not lose the jersey and he was pushing hard to open the gaps and drive home the defeat. He had unleashed his inward concealed strength that you saw in the time trials and the mountains. Each champion, beneath their exterior, somewhere inside themselves, had a store of strength and desire that drove their actions. It was universal. And when they found themselves ahead of the pack, alone on the road, high on a mountain, you could see the power reflected in their eyes and movements and expressions. They came out from the trees and the helicopter showed them from above, the dark green side of the mountain, the thin gray road, the swarming mass of the crowd, and on the road, surrounded by cars and motors, the three riders moving slowly toward the summit.

Pantani was high on the mountain. He was surrounded by the thin air, the crystalline yellow sun, the smooth green slopes, and the snow-covered peaks against the blue sky. The crowd was the largest of the whole Tour and they closed over the climb forming a solid cheering wall, parting only at the last moment to reveal the road leading upward. It was a mob. In 1975 they punched Merckx as he climbed the Puy-du-Dome, and once they brought Parra to a standstill on L'Alpe d'Huez. Pantani came up the narrow corridor, standing on the pedals and swinging the handlebars back and forth, his little body lost in the middle of the crowd, with the steady roar of the klaxons and horns and helicopter, the constant swelling swaying motion of the fans, the blurring colors and faces, the jets of water sprayed overhead, and the hands touching him as he passed. He reached the open slopes, and you could see the lines of the drainage barriers and snow breaks below the ski station. Then he passed the first chalets and white apartment blocks of the resort and rounded the last of the twenty-one lacets. The road widened, the crowd was kept back by the barricades, and the motors pulled ahead and showed him from the side, leaned low over the bicycle with his legs driving a high gear and his eyes focused ahead. Behind, looking out of place against the green slopes, were the cable cars and ski lifts. Above were the runs of gravel of the moraine, the high glacier, the steep gray face, and the white snow-covered peak.

Pantani raced down the middle of the road and passed the one kilometer banner. The gap showed at 1:32. He came through the crowded square, took the final corner so fast that he almost overshot the barricades, and swung onto the Avenue Rif-Nel. The avenue was bright white in the sun, with colors along the straight leading to the high metal gantry and Village Arrivée. The team car and motors turned off the straight, and Pantani came down the wide avenue, the crowd cheering, the flags waving, the red car with the flashing lights following behind. He sprinted all the way to the line, driving forward with his face set in a grimace, and then sat down and smiled, punched the air, clapped his hands, and crossed the line. He coasted to a stop in the Village Arrivée, and the reporters and television crews closed over him.

The Avenue Rif-Nel was empty, with yellow papers blowing away across the straight and the crowd silent, watching the final corner. Then Indurain and Zülle and Riis swept around the corner and spread out in the shimmering heat waves on the avenue. When they came closer you could see Indurain sprinting on the front, looking back under his arm and up for the line, his teeth gritted, showing a faint pride and display of strength at the finish. Zülle followed, Riis began to drop back, and Indurain pushed over the last distance and crossed the line at 1:24.

Maduas came in fifth at 1:54. Then Escartin. Then Jalabert. Gotti crashed in the final corner and was passed by Virenque, who placed eighth. Gotti was ninth, Chiappucci was tenth, Rominger was twelfth.

The others finished in groups or alone, turning the corner and coming down the avenue and across the line, the crowd cheering. They rode straight through the finish area to the team buses or stopped over the bicycles, immediately surrounded by the crowd of reporters. The team personnel reached through the crowds, placed the team caps on their heads, and handed them Coca-Cola bottles to hold for the television, and the riders wiped the sweat from their faces and began answering questions.

Finally the last group arrived. They called it the autobus because it followed behind the peloton like a bus in the mountains, making the finish every day just within the time limit, and those who were dropped hoped to catch the bus so that they would not be eliminated. In the autobus were the sprinters, flats riders, domestiques, leaders who had been dropped, riders who were weak or sick or injured, and usually an older captain called the bus driver who knew the mountains, calculated how much time they could lose, and set the pace on the road. When the riders in the autobus crossed the line at L'Alpe d'Huez they knew they had survived the first mountains of the Tour. The next day they would come down from the Alps into central France, and they could stay in the race for a few more days, at least until they reached the Pyrénées.

The victory celebration was held in the Village Arrivée. Near the finish was a great stage draped in yellow, with the Credit Lyonnais signs of the French bank, and the smaller Fiat, PMU, Champion and 2-Sport-3 banners. Standing behind were the Tour director, sponsors, and guests wearing suits, in the center of the stage was a podium, and on the sides of the podium two very beautiful blonde women wearing red Coca-Cola blouses and short red skirts. Pantani came onto the stage and all the people smiled and clapped as he stepped onto the podium. The women gave him the large bouquet of flowers and kissed him on both cheeks, and he held his arms over his head and saluted the crowd, face shining with sweat, eyes wide and excited. The crowd cheered. You could see the cameras flashing as the photographers shot him from below, and he stepped down from the podium and left the stage.

They repeated the presentation for the other jerseys, with only the women and the colors of their blouses and skirts changing, and then they presented the yellow jersey, and there were two new women wearing matching blue blouses and yellow skirts. Indurain walked onto the stage, all the people clapped, and he stepped onto the podium. The two women pulled a clean yellow jersey over his shoulders, handed him the bouquet of flowers, and kissed him on both cheeks, and he raised his arms over his head and saluted the crowd, turning first one way and then the other, with the quiet modest expression on his face and his eyes moving over the masses of people.

After the victory celebration they cleared the Village Arrivée, and crews began to break down the finish. They would pack the gantry, barricades, booms, cameras, tents, podiums, and miles of cables into trucks, and take them down the mountain and on to the next town before morning, where they would repeat the whole sequence for the next stage. On the television screen they showed the overall classification with Indurain in yellow, Zülle in second at 2:27, Riis third at 5:00, Rominger fourth at 8:19, Gotti fifth at 8:20, and Jalabert sixth at 9:16. That was the classification after the first passage of the mountains. Now there were the flat stages across the plain and they would enter the Pyrénées. In the background I could see the smooth green slopes falling away to the valley, and the high snow-covered peaks of the Galibier and Les Deux Alpes. Below were the streams of people and lines of cars on the road as they began the long procession down the mountain.

22

The next morning I woke late, worked until noon, and came home to meet Anne. I had been training hard and she had been working late in San Francisco, and I had not seen her for almost a week. That afternoon we walked up through the city to the cafe. The summer semester had begun and the streets were crowded with people. On Telegraph Avenue vendors lined the sidewalks, the music and clothing stores were open, and the corners were packed with tourists, homeless, prognosticators, and police. There was a market on one of the side streets and a band was playing in the park. We passed the campus and reached the streets that sloped into the hills. From above we could see the city spread in the sun, the white sails dotting the bay, and the Golden Gate bridge in miniature. Everybody seemed to be outdoors enjoying the day, enjoying the summer, enjoying California.

We reached the cafe and sat down on the terrace under the trees. In the spring the street in front of the cafe had been filled with bicycles and cheering crowds. Then it had seemed strange to have the race in the city. Now it seemed strange to have the city without the race. I looked at the empty streets, and I remembered the feeling of cresting the hill past the cafe, racing down the descent, sprinting up the straight for the finish. Anne looked around and sighed.

"This is where it all started," she said. I turned my head sharply and confronted her.

"Where what started?" Anne smiled quickly.

"You know. The whole bicycle racing thing. Winning. Upgrading to the next category. Becoming a professional. This is where you changed." Suddenly I was filled with reproach. So Anne did not understand. And my family did not understand. Only my friends understood why bicycle racing was important. I waited for a moment before I replied.

"First of all," I said, "I haven't changed. I've been racing for a long time. Much longer than I've known you. And I don't want to be a professional. I just want to do my best." Anne laughed.

"It's about much more than doing your best," she said.

"Maybe for you."

"For all of you. You're crazy. You don't care about anything else!"

"At least I care about something! That's more than I can say for you."

Anne looked stunned. Then she reached across the table and took both of my hands.

"If only you could see yourself," she said. "It's all you think about. You wake up in the morning and you ride your bicycle. At night you watch the Tour. We hardly ever spend time together. I just want us to be happy." I remained silent and Anne dropped my hands. She looked away under the trees.

The afternoon had been destroyed. We had fought. I was hurt by what Anne said and spoke out of anger. There was no way to take back the words. Maybe she was right. I was removed from the world. When I walked around the city I thought only of bicycle racing. In my mind I planned the races, added the points I needed to upgrade, and dreamed about the professionals. Bicycle racing was full of action and exciting experience. It seemed more important than anything else in my life. Gradually I was slipping further away from school and my family. I was even slipping further away from Anne.

I took Anne's hand and she smiled and squeezed my hand in return. Without speaking we sat on the terrace watching people pass in the street. The sun had fallen lower over the bay. The city moved around us. Once more we were in love, two people who had found each other, partners to face the world. Finally we left the cafe and started back down the hill toward home.

23

In the evening I walked up to the bar to watch stage eleven of the Tour. It was the middle of the second week and almost seventy riders had abandoned since the start. They showed the small peloton riding away from the Alps down the Romanche Valley, the high gray and white mountains in the background, the green country on the sides, coming down past Grenoble toward the Isere and St. Etienne south of Lyon. At the first intermediate sprint in Veurey-Voroize three riders broke away, several others bridged, and they moved clear. The highest placed was twenty minutes behind overall, and Banesto did not chase. In the break they worked together smoothly, taking long pulls at the front, forming echelons and pacelines, sharing the work in the wind, and by the middle of the stage they had ten minutes on the peloton.

The Isere was covered with rolling green hills, brown fields, vineyards, and old castles high on the hills. The peloton came down the roads past great fields of yellow sunflowers, waving purple heather, and red carnations, the brightly colored jerseys moving in mass above the country. It was hot and they were riding slowly, jerseys open, sleeves and shorts rolled up in the sun, the fans standing along the road in the shade of the few trees or beside the farmhouses watching silently or cheering as the peloton passed. When the riders came through the towns there were crowds and ringing church bells and high arched sprays from the fountains in the squares, and they raced back into the country hazy in the heat.

At the feed zone the helicopter showed them from above on the long straight road, the team cars parked in rows, the soigneurs standing in ranks holding the mussette bags on their outstretched arms. As the riders swept past they slipped their hands through the straps of the mussettes and took the bags in clean swipes. They sat up on the bicycles, slung the straps over their shoulders, slid the mussettes around to the front, and ate what they could of the pastries and fruits and small sandwiches. They used to stop in the towns for food and water. They would fill their bottles from the fountains or hoses brought by the fans, and run into cafes and restaurants, pushing everybody aside and stuffing bottles of water and soda into their pockets while the owners stood smiling and watching, and then they would run back to the road without paying, climb on their bicycles, and chase after the peloton. They called them fugitives of the Tour. Now it was much faster and nobody could stop. Soon the first riders pulled the mussettes over their shoulders, threw the bags to the side, and leaned down over the bicycles, and once more the group stretched into the long line. Behind you could see the motors driving slowly, and the passengers dragging their feet in the road to catch the mussettes and scraps of food discarded by the riders.

Banesto began working to bring back the break. The flats domestiques, Marino Alonso and Aitor Garmendia, came to the front, and then Thomas Davy, Vincente Aparicio, and Rué, but the gap did not fall. Banesto was tired from the heavy climbing in the mountains, the teams with riders in the break would not chase, and the sprinters would not work with the uphill at the finish. The gap showed at eight minutes. When they moved clear in Veurey-Voroize the riders in the break were only thinking of taking the lead on the long stage and showing the jerseys on the television; in the backs of their minds there was always the small outside hope of staying away to the finish, and when they were not caught they began working harder; now all the doubt had disappeared and they were thinking only of their chance to stay away to finish, move up overall, and maybe to win a stage. They were coming toward the last climbs before St. Etienne.

The motors picked them up on the road and I counted Tafi, Breukink of ONCE, Rolf Jaermann and Max Sciandri of MG-Technogym, Frans Maassen of Novell, Rolf Aldag of Telekom, Armand De Las Quevas of Castorama, and Herman Buenahora of Kelme. Breukink had taken the hillclimb time trial at Villard de Lans and placed third overall in the 1990 Tour. Des Las Quevas had won the Etoile de Besseges, a stage of Paris-Nice, and the French championship for Banesto, disappeared for several years, and come back riding for Castorama, taking the small Trophee des Grimpeurs in the spring. Jaermann, with his sharp pointed face and small lean body, had won the Amstel Gold two years before. Sciandri could sprint from a small group and climb well over the moyenne montagne and won something every year. Maassen and Aldag were sprinters, and I knew they hoped the break would stay together until St. Etienne. Buenahora, like most of Kelme, was a climber, and would have to attack on the climbs if he wanted to take the stage.

The break crossed the Rhône and reached the Col de L'Oiellon. Now, on the last climbs, the fight would begin. De Las Quevas came to the front and began driving the pace, Massen and Jaermann were immediately dropped, and Tafi slowly fell behind. They swept into a steep corner and De Las Quevas looked back over his shoulder; behind were Aldag, Sciandri, Buenahora and Breukink, and below the Isere, with the rolling green hills, flat yellow fields, and winding river. De Las Quevas sat down, his shoulders swaying, his old sallow face looking up the road, and they rounded the corner and came up through a forest with the bright yellow sun through the green trees. Buenahora attacked from behind and dove across the road, his head down, his thin brown arms and legs pumping over the bicycle. Breukink jumped hard and sprinted, gaining no ground, Aldag dropped back, and gradually De Las Quevas faded behind, standing on the pedals and weaving back and forth on the road. Only Sciandri could follow, and he bridged to Buenahora, pulled through, and swung in behind. The two came out from the trees, and there were people standing on the side watching with their hands on their hips and their shirts off in the heat. Behind you could see the deep green valley, the burned brown slopes, and the high dark green ridge. The team cars came up and they moved clear on the climb.

Buenahora led with his small brown body and green Kelme jersey hunched over the bicycle, and his dark almost-Indian face looking up the road. He was Colombian like Muñoz. They had a whole different world of cycling in Colombia, with a professional peloton, a calendar of races, and their own Vuelta which went into the Cordillera of the Andes, higher than any mountains in Europe. The Colombians first came over to Europe in the early 80s with the Postobon and Cafe de Colombia teams. They were the first real American cyclists: Ortiz, Herrerra, Parra, Rodriguez. They always rode for Spanish teams, and they were all climbers. Buenahora had taken the summit points over each climb and he looked strong on the Oeillon. He would not want to carry Sciandri to the line, but he would need him on the descent to hold off the peloton. Sciandri would try to stay with Buenahora over the climbs, use him on the descent, and beat him in the sprint.

The two crested the Oeillon, dropped on the short descent, and reached the Col de la Croix de Chaubouret. It was the final climb of the day and Buenahora rode hard at the front, standing on the pedals and swinging the bicycle back and forth, driving all his weight down on each stroke, trying with his last effort to draw the strength out of Sciandri. Sciandri followed behind, holding the wheel of the climber. They came up through the heavy forest on the smooth black road, and then you saw the white sign with the black writing, SOMMET 1KM, the trees fell away, and there was the clearing with the wide flat greens on the sides, the television banners in the grass, the great crowd, and the Champion banner. Buenahora sprinted under the banner taking the points, and they came over the summit and began the long descent to St. Etienne.

The second motor dropped back on the road, picking up first Breukink, Tafi, and Aldag on the Chaubouret, De Las Quevas on the Oeillon, and finally the peloton just crossing the Rhône with a small group chasing behind through the Isere. Banesto was riding on the front and they came up the lower slopes of the Oeillon and around the first steep corner, climbing with an easy rhythm in high gears. They were not chasing hard, and I knew that they had decided to let the break go. Often on the long flat stages between the mountains the leaders did not chase, and the long breaks stayed away to the finish. When they came over the summit the gap showed at seven minutes. The peloton dropped onto the Chaubouret, the two groups came back together, and they crested the summit and began the descent to St. Etienne.

Sciandri was coasting with his head down, his hands together near the stem, his body hanging off the back of the saddle in a low aerodynamic tuck. Then he sat up and began pedaling, and several lengths behind was Buenahora, crouched over the bicycle with his jersey blown flat and his legs spinning fast. They came out from the forest and the smooth green slopes spread away, the road leading down through the hills. Below was the Loire, and in the distance the old white city of St. Etienne.

St. Etienne was one of the famous cities of the Tour, once the center of the steel industry and bicycle manufacturing, where many races had finished over the years. As they came down into the Loire the hills were covered with orchards and vineyards, and then there were chalets, low stone walls, and thick green trees over the road. They passed the five kilometer banner and Sciandri dropped back from the front, drank, poured water over his shoulders and threw the bottle to the side of the road, and then drew alongside Buenahora and asked for more water. Buenahora handed a bottle across and Sciandri again drank, poured the water over his shoulders and threw the bottle to the side. They are still working together, I thought. They would keep working on the descent, through the outskirts, and into the city, and then in the last kilometer they would begin the end game. Sciandri took the front, they came out from the trees past the first houses, and the road turned down toward the city.

Finally they reached the long straight boulevards on the outskirts of St. Etienne, and the narrow streets with the old buildings, rows of houses, and heavy cheering crowds. They were still descending toward the center of the city, and they both moved over to the gutter and slowed. Now they were no longer working together, and you could see them watching each other closely and looking up the road for the final turn. There were always the two-up sprints in the Tour, with the riders who had been away in the long breaks jockeying for position in the last kilometer. The finish came after a right hand turn and a short steep climb. Sciandri would take the sprint from a long way out to overpower the smaller climber; Buenahora would hold himself back and attack on the hill where he had the jump. Buenahora took the front, riding slowly, and you could see him ducking his head and looking back under his arm. Then Sciandri came through, standing on the pedals and swinging the bicycle from side to side, looking back over his shoulder, and there was the tension of the two riders approaching the final turn with their having been no time checks on the descent, not knowing how far behind the peloton was, hoping they would not suddenly appear in the streets and sweep past the break.

They passed the one kilometer banner, swept through a wide open flat intersection, and came around the final turn onto the climb. The road was steep and there were rows of heavy green trees on the sides, high white apartment buildings, and ranks of people lining the straight.

Sciandri immediately moved left against barricades, standing on the pedals and swinging the handlebars back and forth, looking over his shoulder, with Buenahora close on his wheel. They came up the curving climb and Sciandri raced along the barricades, his head turned slightly to the side, watching the road and the finish. Finally Sciandri began to sprint, moving toward the center of the road. Buenahora was out of the saddle, his body thrashing back and forth over the bicycle, but he could not pass, and Sciandri sat up, looked back once more, turned and smiled, raised his arms to the crowd, and crossed the line.

The three from the break came into St. Etienne and up the climb with Aldag taking the sprint for third place. De Las Quevas finished alone in sixth. Then the peloton came around the final turn and up the climb with two Novells on the front and Jalabert, Riis, and Abdujaparov following behind. Whoever won the sprint would take the green jersey. The Novells drove up the left and swung off and dropped back, and Jalabert came through on the right sprinting hard with Riis on his wheel. Abdujaparov surged forward and swerved sharply taking the wheel from Riis, drew even with Jalabert, and the two sprinted down the straight along the barricades and threw their bicycles over the line.

Jalabert won the sprint and kept the green jersey by a few points. Buenahora took the red number of the Prix de la Combativite for the summit points and his attack on the Oiellon. They showed the victory celebrations and the coverage ended.

Anne had begun working late in the city, and I knew she was not at home. I sat at the crowded bar, thinking about the finish. The overall had not changed, and now, after the Alps, I did not think that they could beat Indurain. They could not beat him in the time trials, they could not beat him in the mountains, and they could not beat him on the flats. The race was not over. There were still the Pyrénées. But I knew that Indurain had won the Tour.

24

It was Friday. Finally the week was over. I was frustrated from training and I still had not placed in the races. I did not want to think about the weekend and I walked up to the bar to watch the Tour. When the coverage began I was suddenly captivated. Jalabert had broken away through the Loire, gained ten minutes on the peloton, and was the new yellow jersey on the road. They showed the break coming through one of the small towns along the course, the streets packed with people, blue-white-red flags overhead, the crowds cheering on the national holiday. It was Bastille Day. Jalabert raced past toward the finish at the World War II airfield in Mende.

That was why the Tour was so interesting. The race always changed on the road. You could never predict exactly what would happen or how the race would develop. That morning as they left St. Etienne there was an attack on the Côte de Saint Maurice. Jalabert countered and moved clear with Dario Bottaro of Gewiss-Ballan. Mauri came across, Jalabert took the intermediate sprint in Chaumalix, and when they learned that another group including Stephens was bridging they waited and the three became six. By attacking before the sprint and sending their riders across one by one ONCE surprised the other teams. The race broke apart through the difficult terrain, Banesto was caught behind, and when the motors picked them up on the road Indurain was chasing alone at the head of the peloton.

They showed the break with the two ONCE domestiques working on the front, and Jalabert, Bottaro, Andrea Peron of Motorola, and Massimo Podenzana of Brecialat in line, surrounded by the tightly grouped motors and cars. They were riding south through the Loire into Ardeche and the county was slowly changing, heavy green ridges and bare brown and yellow fields on the sides, the plain dotted with dry brush and sparse trees, looking, in the shimmering heat, like Africa or a desert country, until they came closer and I saw that the brush were rounds of hay, the trees were arranged in straight rows, and there were small towns with red roofs and white churches against the burned country.

Banesto slowly brought the peloton back together, and the gap showed at 10:36. Jalabert was 9:16 behind overall. Banesto had to bring the gap under nine minutes or Indurain would lose the jersey. Again the team with riders in the break would not chase, and the sprinters would not work with the long climb at the finish. Banesto would have to call in all their favors; they were one of the largest teams in the peloton, they were sponsored by the Spanish national bank, and over the years they had given many of the other teams support on the road, stage wins, or small races for the promise of assistance in the future. Now, in the caravan, Unzue was on the phone talking to the directors of the other teams, buying and selling the race. It never felt right when you heard about the deals and the money making, but it was a business, and soon you saw Gewiss-Ballan come up riding for Riis in third place, Novell riding for Abdujaparov and the green jersey, and smaller teams that had no clear reason for working, MG-Technogym, Polti, AKI, and Chazal, and slowly the time gap began to fall.

The break raced into the small white town of Arouux and came down through a light green forest back to the plain. Neil Stephens was leading the break, his short body working over the bicycle, his long hair streaming back in the wind, his tan face looking up the road. They reached the Côte de Chapal, Stephens dropped back, and Mauri came through on the front.

On the Côte de Chapal the road went straight over the hills with the crowd standing in lines, high green banks on the sides, and grassy yellow slopes spreading away toward the summit. Mauri was climbing fast out of the saddle, and slowly Stephens began to fall behind. The gap opened and he drew himself forward and closed the gap. Again the gap opened and again Stephens drew himself forward and closed the gap. For the last time the gap opened and Bottaro and Podenzana sprinted past. The motors fell back with Stephens, showing him from the side, head down, arms pulling, legs straining. The others went up the climb in a driving line. Stephens was one of the few Australians in the peloton. He was a great domestique and he always gave everything he could. He had bridged after Chaumalix, pulled Jalabert through the Loire against the work of Indurain and Banesto and all the other teams, and now his work was done for the day. He would wait for the peloton, find a place in the middle of the group, and ride in slowly to recover so that he could work for the team the next day, and the next, and then in the Pyrénées.

The motor swung around Stephens and raced up the climb and caught the five coming up through the corridor of the crowd. Mauri was still on the front and they were out of the saddles working hard, the bicycles going from side to side, the fans leaning into the road cheering and waving flags. Ahead was the dark green line of the trees over the summit. They came through the break in the trees, and began the long descent into the Lot River valley.

The peloton reached the Chapal and caught Stephens and crested the summit. The gap showed at 9:07. Jalabert was no longer the yellow jersey on the road. The peloton was closer, but there was still the final climb to Mende. The break was coming down through the hills, Mauri still on the front, head down, body stretched long and low over the bicycle, spinning fast. Jalabert was coasting in the draft, and the others were following behind. Slowly they pulled ahead of the motors and the helicopter picked them up lower coming out of the hills, the five riders moving in line against the burned brown country. They ran out in the valley, crossed the Lot River, and reached the town of Mende.

Mauri led the break through the town onto the Monte de Causee de Mende. Jalabert had been away since the first intermediate sprint, and all through the stage there was the anticipation waiting for him to attack. Now they had reached the final climb. The road began to rise, turned left into a forest, and came out far above on the plateau to the airfield and finish.

Mauri held his long sprint onto the climb, and you could see the rhythm of his pedaling change with the last final effort and giving of himself before the finish. Then Jalabert attacked from behind and sprinted away up the road. He dove into the sharp left hand corner and turned and looked back over his shoulder. Bottaro was five bicycle lengths down and the others were farther behind. Both of them were out of the saddle racing hard, and they rounded a corner and climbed a straight along steep green banks. Jalabert swept around a second corner and looked back again. Bottaro had dropped back and the gap opened to six, seven, eight lengths. Finally the red car and team car pulled around, and Jalabert moved clear. It was amazing about Jalabert. Last year he had only been a sprinter, and nobody would have picked him to win Paris-Nice or Liège-Bastogne-Liège or the overall in the Tour. Then, on the stage to Armentieres, sprinting at the head of the peloton, he crashed in the final meters. You still saw the pictures of him sitting with the stunned expression on his face, blood running down his jersey, bicycles and riders scattered across the straight. When Jalabert came back from that crash he was no longer a pure sprinter, but had become a Classics rider and leader as well, and now he was racing for the yellow jersey. The first motor showed Jalabert out of the saddle, body swaying back and forth, face pale and impassive, cheeks slack, mouth slightly open, eyes hidden behind dark sunglasses, the only sign of exertion the sheen of sweat over his skin and the fast swinging rhythm of his arms and legs. The gap was eight minutes. Below, through the trees, you could see the white houses of the town, the burned brown hills, and the white line of the peloton.

The peloton crossed the Lot River valley and raced through Mende onto the final climb. Banesto and Gewiss-Ballan were working on the front, and Carrera and Festina came up with Pantani and Virenque riding side by side. Pantani pulled ahead, Virenque dropped back, and Zülle attacked. They all swept around the first corner and went up the climb under the trees.

They came through the forest with the cheering crowd and sun bright and hot on the road. Zülle was setting the pace, Indurain and Riis were following behind, and ahead you could see the small figure of Pantani moving up through the crowd. It was the first time it looked like they were hurting Indurain. You could see the faint strained expression on his face, the smooth driving power was gone, and he was standing on the pedals fighting the gear. He must be tired from the long chase, I thought. Gradually Zülle slowed, Indurain and Riis drove past, and Riis turned and looked back over his shoulder. Zülle fell behind with his head down, body swaying from side to side, legs straining, and the crowd closed over him on the road. They had dropped him. Maybe Riis would move into second or Jalabert or Pantani would take third. They were spread all over the climb and there would be no way to tell until the finish.

Jalabert came out of the forest with the fans standing in lines forming the narrow corridor and the flags and banners waving overhead. His face was still blank, his body was working hard over the bicycle, and his skin was shining with sweat. Then you could see the Champion banner above the crowd, and he rode under the banner and over the crest of the climb, shifting gears and leaning forward without breaking the rhythm of his pedaling. He had reached the summit plateau; on the sides the slopes spread away to the dark line of the woods, and beyond you could see the few white clouds and the clear blue sky.

Jalabert raced across the plateau and reached the airfield. He swept through the final turn, with the cars and motors banking in formation, coming upright, and spreading out in the shimmering heat waves on the runway. The runway was long and straight and wide. Jalabert came down the middle of the runway, looking small, with the green jersey fluttering in the wind over the plateau. Usually they did not cheer strongly for Jalabert because he rode for Spanish teams, but he had stayed away for the whole stage, he had been the yellow jersey on the road, and he had won on Bastille Day, and the roar was louder even than on L'Alpe d'Huez. The fans leaned over the barricades and chanted his name, beat on the boards with their fists, and waved the small yellow Tour flags and the huge French flags. Jalabert stood on the pedals and sprinted for a few strokes and then looked back over his shoulder; the motors and team cars had been pulled and far down the runway you could see Podenzana alone keeping close to the barricades. Jalabert turned around and his face broke into a smile. He sat up on the bicycle, closed the collar of his jersey, and straightened his cap for the sponsors. Then he looked back once more, punched the air, raised both arms over his head, and punched the air again. Finally he sat up on the bicycle, bent his elbows bringing his two hands to his mouth, kissed his hands, raised his arms in a salute, threw his head back, and crossed the line, the red car following slowly behind.

Podenzana came down the runway and crossed the line twenty-nine seconds after Jalabert. In the distance you could see another rider on the right, another, and another, spread out with the cars and motors. Bottaro finished thirteen seconds behind Podenzana, Mauri six seconds later leading a formation of motors, then Peron alone, veering sharply as he crossed the line.

They picked up Pantani near the summit of the climb. He was coming up through the corridor of the crowd with his bald head gleaming with sweat, his brow furrowed from the effort, his thin arms and legs working over the bicycle. Behind, surrounded by the crowd, were Indurain and Riis. Indurain was leading, and when they came over the summit the split showed at 4:00. Jalabert had taken third place. We would have to wait for Zülle to know about second. On the descent Indurain caught Pantani and went straight past, Riis pulled through, racing to distance himself from Zülle, and they crossed the plateau, reached the airfield, and swept through the final turn onto the runway with the sound rising from the crowd. Indurain and Riis worked together down the runway, and then Indurain began to lead out the sprint. Riis came around on the right, Pantani jumped from behind and sprinted toward the center with his head down and his elbows out and the bicycle going from side to side, and crossed the line for sixth at 5:41. Zülle came down the runway alone and crossed the line at 5:48.

The rest of the peloton came slowly down the runway and over the line in a large group. Indurain kept the yellow jersey, Zülle held onto second place, and Jalabert took third from Riis. It had been a wonderful stage on Bastille Day, with the surprise break and close racing and win for all of France, and there was the deal-making in the caravan and uncertain motives as they chased through the Loire, but nobody would remember that after the Tour. They will not even remember tomorrow, I thought. They will only remember Jalabert riding into third place and winning the stage on Bastille Day. He would have to hold onto third place. They were going into the Pyrénées.

From the high plateau above Mende you could not yet see the mountains, but the following day and the day after, as they rode south through Aveyron and Tarn, the broken line of the Pyrénées would rise across the plain on the horizon. Then the Tour would become truly hard. The first day in the Pyrénées they would ride one hundred miles over four mountains to Guzet Niege; the following day they would ride one hundred and thirty miles over six mountains to Cauterets, the longest stage of the Tour.

It was only the second week and already the average speed was faster than ever before. It seemed as if they would keep going and never stop. The unrelenting momentum of the Tour and the pressure I felt to upgrade became entangled like nightmares in my mind and I was overcome with fatigue. The exciting feeling of racing was gone. The bar was dark and loud and filled with smoke. I turned away from the counter, pushed through the crowd, and went out onto the avenue. Outside the air was clear and there was a light breeze coming down from the hills. It felt good to be out of the bar away from the crowds. Anne had gone away for the weekend. I had promised to meet her in the city but I was too tired to travel into San Francisco. When I reached home I lay face down on my bed without removing my clothes, and fell fast asleep.

25

The weekend the Tour went into the Pyrénées there was a road race in Great Central Valley. We left the city on Sunday morning, drove over the pass, and came down to the course in the hills along the western border of the valley. The day was hot and dry and the country was covered by a thick haze of dust. Starting out I rode in the middle of the pack with my jersey open and my shorts and sleeves rolled up in the sun. Already my legs were heavy and I felt faint in the heat. I reached down and drank, and then moved up the line. I wanted to be at the front when we started the climb.

The long winding procession came down through the valley and turned onto a smaller road that led into the hills. The pack slowed and there were the sounds of shifting gears as we began to climb. I slid back in the saddle and moved my hands to the tops of the bars, pulling rhythmically with my back and shoulders against the grade. Looking ahead I saw Chris at the front of the pack. He had been waiting all season and finally we had reached the long summer road races. I knew that he wanted to do well so that we could all race together in the Pro/I-IIs. I only hoped that the race did not break apart so quickly that I was dropped. The road grew steeper, winding upward over slopes of thick gray brush, and coming out above in the grassy open country. I was breathing hard, sweat was rising on my skin, and there was a growing pain in my my legs. We swung round the first corner and I stood on the pedals to stretch my legs and looked back down the climb. The pack was stretched into a long line and the caravan was following behind. I sat down and held the steady pace. Then, gradually, I began to fall back through the pack.

What was it about climbs? I could ride on the flats and I could sprint, but I could not climb. You are too big to climb, I thought. No, that's not true. Indurain and Zülle and Riis are big and they can climb. But they can't sprint, not like Cipollini, who, looking at them, has the same tall lean powerful body. There were climbers, sprinters, and flats riders. There were also riders who could do everything, like Jalabert or John, but I was not one of them. I was a sprinter. I had the sudden, fearless, jumping-on-the-pedals, bursting-from-the-pack speed at the end of a race, but I could not climb. In the mountains the country was most beautiful, the races were most dramatic, and I loved the feelings of climbing, driving up the straights, sweeping around the corners, coming over the crests and dropping on the descents, but I never climbed well in the races. I always started near the front, fell back through the pack, and was dropped. Now we had reached the climbs. They were just hills along the side of the valley. The only real mountains where we rode were the Sierra Nevada, the Santa Cruz range along the coast, and Mount Diablo. The Tour had gone back into the mountains. Maybe they would beat Indurain. Don't think of that now, I told myself. Don't think of the Tour. You are riding your own race. You have to stay with the pack and place in the sprint. You have to upgrade. Just don't get dropped. Make it over the crest and it will be downhill to the finish.

As we climbed the slopes fell away and there was the growing feeling of height and openness over the valley. We had climbed above the dust into the clear air and I could see the high broken line of the Sierra on the horizon. Around me the riders were working over the bicycles, their faces shining with sweat, their shoulders swaying back and forth, their mouths open breathing hard. We swept around a switchback and the front sprinted up the straight. I stood on the pedals to follow and suddenly the pain was sharp and I sat down heavily and slowed. My chest was heaving and my heart was pounding and there was the hot spreading weakness in my legs. Reaching for my shift lever I saw that I was already in the lowest gear, and I turned around and looked back down the road. The end of the line was close, and I could see the official motors and follow cars driving slowly behind. I leaned forward and smoothed my pedaling, but I was slipping backward down the line and riders were passing on both sides. Finally the last rider came around and I jumped on the pedals and lunged forward to catch his wheel. He slowly pulled away, and there was the desperate, rushing, slipping-away feeling, and the voice in the back of my mind saying you are getting dropped, you are getting dropped, but I could not ride any faster. The motors and follow cars passed with the loud revving of the engines. Then they were gone and I was alone. It was quiet and I could hear my breaths high in my throat and the wind moving through the grass over the slopes. The small caravan and pack receded up the road, rounded a corner, and disappeared.

You were dropped, I thought. On the climb during the hardest part of the season you were not strong enough. I looked down at my legs turning slowly over the pedals; they were not strong enough. At least you rode as hard as you could. That was something. It was not often that you gave everything and either succeeded or failed. Most of the time in bicycle racing you lost. Even the best champions lost many more races than they won.

I sat up and took a long drink of water, and then I poured the bottle over my head and shoulders, and settled into a steady pace that I could hold for the length of the climb. You had to ride your own rhythm on the climbs. If you tried to ride too fast you would fall behind and never recover. Maybe you can get into a small group, I thought. There was still the descent and the flat run through the valley. Turning in the saddle I looked back down the climb and saw two riders coming up the switch-backs below and a third farther behind, and I slowed so that they would catch me and I would have somebody to work with on the descent.

The two reached me and passed without speaking and I dropped in behind. They were teammates: one was tall and dark and was breathing hard, and the other was short and heavy and was doing all the work. Then the third rider reached us and I saw that is was the big sprinter from San Diego with whom I had almost won the Santa Rosa road race in the spring. He had crashed, his shorts were torn and bloody, and he was pedaling harder with one leg and favoring the side on which he had fallen. It was not like other sports where they stopped the clock when you crashed; they went on without you, and you had to get back on your bicycle and keep riding. When I saw that he had lost his bottles I reached down and handed my bottle across. He drank a small amount, poured the water over his leg washing away the dried blood and dust, and handed the bottle back. We went up the road toward the crest of the climb.

With the others the pace was steady, and slowly the strength came back into my legs. We crested the open brown summit flat. On the other side were the rolling hills and oak country leading west. Behind was the Great Central Valley. I sat up and closed my jersey and we began the descent.

From the ridge the road went down in a long straight. I coasted with my hands on the hoods, my legs resting, the wind building as we gained speed. Then we were working together in fast rotation, tucked over the bicycles, taking short turns at the front, pulling off hard and dropping back. We came down from the hills and the country spread out on the sides. Then, far below, I could see the small caravan and the pack on the road. Maybe you will catch them, I thought. Maybe you will finish with the front group. Maybe you will place in the sprint.

I remembered the race in Italy where I was dropped from the pack over the last steep climb. I came up through a forest with thick green trees and bright sun and people from the town standing in lines cheering and shouting and throwing water into the road. On the descent I passed an official waving a red flag shouting *rallentare, rallentare*, slow down, where there were rocks and gravel in a corner. Reaching a wide green plateau I chased alone over the country, came down through the brown earth fields, and finally caught the pack. We turned onto a long straight bordered by rows of plane trees and a motor drove slowly up the line filming the race for a local television station. You caught the front group that day, I thought. I knew we would catch the pack in the valley.

We passed the caravan at high speed on the descent, coming up behind the cars, drawing alongside, and pulling away with the sound of the engines fading. Ahead I could see the white mass of the pack, then the bright colors of the jerseys, and then the individual riders. Finally we reached the back of the group and, carrying my speed, I went up the line and moved into the pack. Then I coasted, relieved to have made the pack. You caught them, I thought. You were dropped on the climb but you rode your own rhythm, recovered, worked hard on the descent, and fought back into the race. The road came down from the hills and we ran out in the fields and turned through the valley.

In the valley it was hot and dusty and the wind was blowing hard. We were riding away from the hills and I knew that we were close to the finish. Reaching down I drank the last of my water, and then stood on the pedals to stretch my legs and went up to the front. Ahead was a long straight with heat waves shimmering in the distance. There were no other groups in sight and I turned around and looked back down the road. The pack was all together and the others were sitting up on the bicycles with their jerseys open and their faces streaked with sweat and dust. They were riding slowly in easy gears. You did not catch the front group, I thought. You are riding with the last group. When I realized that I had reached the last group there was the sudden feeling of defeat, and I pulled to the side and dropped back through the pack. There was no reason to keep going. There were only six places and they did not give out points for finishing last. At least you'll finish, I told myself, but I knew that there were only the places and the points and that nothing else mattered. We rode down the valley away from the hills. I crossed the finish line at the back of the group.

26

On Monday there was a rest day in the Tour and they laid over in Saint Girons. I woke late in the morning, worked through the day, and came home in the evening. Anne had not returned from the weekend, and I waited for her at home and went to sleep early. The next day it was cold and overcast. I worked in the morning and went for a long slow ride in the afternoon. On the other side of the hills it was sunny and hot, and I rode home in the evening. Anne had still not returned. I called her in the city, waited until midnight, and then walked up to the bar to watch the Tour. It was the stage to Cauterets.

The bar was crowded with people, the lights were low, and the music was loud. I pushed through the crowd and sat down at the counter. Over the weekend the peloton had crossed Aveyron and Tarn and Garonne on the long run past Toulouse, and reached the Pyrénées. Pantani had won at Guzzet Niege. He was the first rider in a long time to win stages in both the Alps and Pyrénées, and I thought again that he was the best climber in the Tour.

They started out from the town of St. Girons. It was bright and sunny and they rode through the old quarter with the narrow streets, tan houses and red roofs, strings of green and yellow flags, and people standing under the archways and in the doorways and windows cheering and waving handkerchiefs. Leaving town they crossed an old stone bridge over a wide shallow river, and came into Ariege, green and overgrown, with yellow and brown fields on the sides. Watching them ride slowly down the valley there was a feeling like setting out for a long ride in the country, with a faint edge of foreboding as they entered the mountains. They passed an intermediate sprint, and began the first climb of the day, the Portet d'Aspet.

That day they would ride up a long valley, following in rough parallel the frontier of Spain, with each mountain carrying them higher, until they reached the Pont-d'Espagne. Now, on the Portet d'Aspet, they rode slowly, coming up over the light green forested slopes in the bright sun, the caravan following behind. Approaching the summit, Cornillet of Chazal attacked, and on the opposite side of the peloton Virenque pushed to the front, cut across the road, and sprinted up the climb. Virenque caught and passed Cornillet, took the sprint under the Champion banner, and began the long descent. A few moments later the peloton came over the summit and started down the descent.

The motors followed Virenque and Bruno Cornillet, showing them crouched over the bicycles with their heads down and their backs low and their legs spinning, and they came through the heavy forest, banking first in one direction and then the other, the wheels of the follow cars squealing around the corners, the speed of the motor on the screen passing forty miles per hour, fifty miles per hour, sixty miles per hour. Then the motor braked sharply and dropped back, and the two gradually pulled away and disappeared. Lower on the mountain the motor picked up the peloton coming out from the trees around a corner. There had been a crash and the team cars were stopped in line. There was a Mapei-GB sitting in the road, a Kelme jumping up and stumbling over a bicycle, and a Motorola lying in the road. Farther down a TVM rider was standing and picking up his bicycle, a mechanic was holding wheels in his hands, and several people were running to the side where somebody had gone over into a ravine. The peloton streamed past in the background, and then they were gone and the road was clear.

When they showed the peloton again they were riding slowly through the fields in the valley. They were waiting for those who crashed. At the beginning of the long stages in the mountains the peloton often kept the pace low so that riders who had been dropped could chase back on. At the bottom of the screen the small window came up with the words, *Chute*, crash, *Les Blessés*, the injured, and the names of the riders: Dirk Ballinger of TVM, Dante Rezze of AKI, Fabio Casartelli of Motorola. Only three names, I thought. The others must be chasing. The peloton came down the valley and turned onto the Col de Mente, still riding all together, and they swept around the first corner and went up past steep yellow rock faces and heavy green growth. As they rode farther south into the Pyrénées the country changed. In the valleys there were no longer green and yellow fields but brown rolling foothills, the roads were not smooth and graded with embankments and lacets, but narrow and white and rough, and there was not high green alpine country but dry brown burned land, broken gray rocks, bare cuts of earth, runs of gravel, and finally great towering faces and black peaks covered with snow. They called it the *casse desert* or high desert. On the Col de Mente they had not yet reached the casse desert. They came up through the pastures and pine forests, Virenque took the sprint under the Champion banner, and they went over the summit and began the descent.

The peloton rode through Luchon and reached the Col de Peyresourde, and at the bottom of the climb Virenque attacked and moved clear with Buenahora. The helicopter showed the two rounding a switchback with a group of five coming up behind, and then three more bridged and there were ten. The motors picked them up on the road and I counted Virenque, Buenahora, Dufaux, Chiappucci, Stephens,

Escartin, Bo Hamburger, Bolts, Oscar Pellicioli, and Miguel Arroyo. That was the break. Dufaux would ride for Virenque, none of the others were high overall, and there were enough teams represented that the peloton would not chase. They were working in line on the climb, and as they came up through one of the small high mountain towns the window showed with the names, Ballinger, Rezze, Casartelli, and the words, Hopital, Tarbes. They had taken the riders who crashed to the hospital in Tarbes. Their Tour was over, and I hoped they would come back for the fall Classics or the Vuelta later in the season.

The break was high in the Pyrénées. Ahead in the distance you could see Val Louron, and across the valley to the south the parallel ridge of the Maladeta and the Pico Posets of the Spanish frontier. Then the road turned and you could see the French side, with the burned yellow slopes, white rocks breaking through the grass, and the feeling of height and emptiness looking down into the valley. Bolts, Pellicioli, and Arroyo had been dropped, Mauri and Aparicio had come up from the peloton, and Dufaux was riding on the front. Then, as they approached the summit, Virenque stood on the pedals and attacked. He moved clear and they showed him climbing fast out of the saddle surrounded by the motors and red car. It was very early to attack. They were only on the second mountain, and Virenque had Dufaux in the break. Maybe he was scared of Escartin or Chiappucci. There were still the climbs of the Aspin, the Tourmalet, and Cauterets, but Virenque was alone, and he came up through the crowd and under the banner and over the summit. On the descent he crouched low over the bicycle, pulled away from the motors, and went down the mountain toward the valley.

Virenque ran out in the valley town of Arreau, crossed the Garonne River, and reached the Col d'Aspin. The road led up through a forest of young trees with thin white trunks and light green leaves and flickering yellow sun. He was climbing with steady rhythm, and when the crowd saw the French rider leading the Tour in the red-and-white mountain jersey they closed over the road shouting and cheering and waving flags.

Then, at the bottom of the screen, the window came up with the name, Fabio Casartelli, age, 24, country, Italy, team, Motorola, and the word, *Morte,* dead. They showed the crash on the Portet d'Aspet, and I saw the Mapei-GB sitting in the road, the Kelme jumping up and stumbling, and the TVM rider farther down the road. Rezze must have been the one who went over into the ravine, I thought. And that must be Fabio Casartelli. The Motorola rider was lying on the road in the sun, facing the low white concrete blocks at the edge of the ravine. One of his arms was folded under his body and the other was thrown back over his legs, his knees were drawn toward his chest, his head was bent forward, and his bicycle was beside him on the road.

The only other rider who actually died on the road in the Tour was Tom Simpson. That was in 1967 on the Ventoux. He collapsed near the summit, they put him back on the bicycle and he kept riding, and then he came off again, and they could not revive him. He died on the mountain. Casartelli had won the Olympic road race in 1992. Now he was dead. Again they showed the crash on the Portet d'Aspet with Casartelli lying in the road, and watching in the bar, knowing that he was dead, the others talking and laughing around me, there was a cold chill over my body and the hollow empty feeling of the race.

They cut back to Virenque racing at the front, standing on the pedals and swinging the bicycle back and forth, his face shining with sweat, his eyes wide and excited, the crowd shouting and cheering and running alongside waving flags. The motors and red car and team car were following slowly behind. They do not know that Casartelli died, I thought. It would have been announced over Radio Tour, and they would know in the caravan, but it would not have gone out over the public radio or live television feed, and we only got it afterward. It was better for the riders, but in the caravan they would have to drive with it all the way to the finish.

The yellow motor came up and gave Virenque the gap on the green chalkboard: the splits showed at 1:00 to the poursuivants and 3:20 to the peloton. They were still running the time checks. The race would not stop. Virenque came out of the forest through the heavy crowd and one fan ran alongside holding a great French flag. The flag flapped and billowed, covering the camera, showing only the blue-white-red colors, drawing back to reveal Virenque, racing up through the crowd over the summit of the Aspin. On the other side you could see the long brown hazy valley and higher massed mountains. He sat up and closed his jersey, leaned down over the bicycle, and began the descent.

The motors picked up the chase group on the Aspin. They were climbing through the forest with Chiappucci on the front and the others following behind. Stephens had dropped back, and Aparicio was riding at the back of the line. When they came out of the forest the helicopter showed them from above, and you could see the riders moving up through the crowd, the fans running alongside, the flags and banners waving over the road, and the 2-Sport-3 banners spread on the sides so that they could be seen from the helicopter. Maybe it is all just a show, I thought. Maybe it is all arranged for the television. Maybe they are just advertisements and race for the money. For some of them it must be about money, I knew, but for all of them it could not be or always have been about money. Each of them must have loved bicycle racing at some point. They could not ride and give of themselves the way they did unless they loved racing. Think of Indurain on L'Alpe d'Huez, Jalabert on Bastille Day, or Stephens on the Chapal. It was a professional sport, but it was not just a business. It could not be just a business, I told myself. It was not worth that. They were approaching the summit, the crowds were larger, and there were more 2-Sport-3 banners, and the Champion banner over the road. They came up through the crowd and over the summit onto the descent.

Virenque crossed the valley and raced through the town of St. Marie de Campan and reached the Col du Tourmalet. It was a long climb, and they showed him coming up through the heavy forest on the lower slopes. The Tourmalet was the highest mountain in the Tour. It was not really a summit but a high pass between two peaks. I remembered the pictures of the Tourmalet from the first part of the century, the old rough dirt road, the riders climbing slowly or walking their bicycles wearing wool jerseys and leggings and goggles, tires wrapped around their shoulders, faces covered with brown dust, the few open cars and motors that were the whole Tour following behind, surrounded by the great high open barren mountain. Now the road over the pass was paved and there was the La Mongie station at the summit. Virenque came out of the forest, the green and yellow slopes spreading away toward the higher country, and you could see the great crowd above lining the road.

The motor dropped back and picked up the chase group lower on the Tourmalet. Chiappucci, Mauri, Escartin, Dufaux and Buenahora were riding together in a small group, Hamburger and Aparicio were following behind, and farther back Rué and Davy were leading the peloton through the forest. When they came out from the trees Riis stood on the pedals and attacked, and he caught and dropped Aparicio, and went on alone. He was racing to take back third place. The peloton reached the long tunnels with the sloped half-roofs and the road shadowed on one side and open to the sun on the other, and when they came out of the tunnels Rué and Davy dropped back, and Zülle attacked and moved clear on the road tracking along the side of the mountain. Indurain slowly pulled away from the others, caught and passed Zülle, and the two went up the climb after Riis.

Virenque was high on the mountain. The helicopter showed him from above with the gray towering faces, green and yellow slopes, and road winding upward lined by thousands of fans. Then they switched to the motors and you saw the one rider coming up through the crowd, racing faster and faster, climbing out of the saddle with his body swaying back and forth, legs driving down, face shining with sweat, mouth open breathing hard, eyes wide and excited.

Look at him, I thought. He was in a trance. I wonder if it's true what they say about the drugs. You heard about them racing *chaud* or hot. You heard about the syringes in the small cut-off cigar tubes in their jersey pockets, the injections in their shoulder or buttocks, and the treatments from the team doctors in the hotels. You heard about the medicines the soigneurs gave on the massage tables, the suitcases full of pills and prescriptions, and the black market accounts kept by the teams with the prize winnings. There were drug controls, but the positive tests were always covered up, and the commisaires, directors, and sponsors looked the other way. Watching them climb in the second week, high in the mountains, it was hard to believe that they were not taking something. It must be true, I thought. They were paid to win races and the stakes were high. Thinking that way did not feel right, but I knew that it was not black and white, and most of all I understood that the riders did what they needed to survive and win.

Indurain and Zülle caught Riis. The three had been together for the whole Tour. Indurain led with Zülle and Riis following behind like his shadows. They came up through the great crowd on the road winding over the burned slopes toward the summit. As they approached the crowd swelled forward and heaved back like a wave, the people cheering and shouting and running alongside, and you saw the yellow flags, French flags, Italian and Danish and Swiss flags, and all the flags from the small provinces and towns; the black-and-white Breton flags, the small blue flags with the yellow cross, the blue flags with the sword, the white flags with the crest and shield, and then, higher, the red-yellow-red Spanish flags, and most of all the red-green-white Basque flags. The Basque fans had crossed the Pyrénées from Navarre to meet Indurain, and they stood in groups, bareheaded or wearing black berets, their faces painted red-green-white, singing and dancing and shouting *aupa*, *aupa*. They all ran into the road and crouched down holding the flags low and furled, and then jumped back and unfurled the flags shaking them close to the ground like they were driving bulls as Indurain, Zülle, and Riis passed.

Virenque was approaching the summit. On the narrow road the crowd stood in lines, forming the heavy solid cheering corridor, and you could see the Garde Republicaine in blue-and-white uniforms, leaning back against the fans with their legs spread wide and their arms outstretched to keep the road clear. Behind, over the high open slopes, were the cables and towers and ski lifts of the La Mongie station. Virenque came up through the corridor, curved left past the stone inn with the patio and cafe tables and wooden railing, and sprinted under the Champion banner and over the Tourmalet Pass at the highest point in the Tour. On the other side of the pass the road fell in a long straight. The valley dropped away below, on the right and left were great towering faces and black rock peaks laced with snow, and from the peaks fans of gravel and boulders spread down to the road. The country was dry and bare, a strong wind was blowing up from the valley raising dust, and the sun was bright and hot. The Tour had reached the casse dessert. Virenque sat up and closed his jersey, and then crouched down over the bicycle, and dropped from the pass on the road toward Bareges and Luz-St. Sauveur.

Chiappucci, Escartin, and Buenahora came over the Tourmalet Pass together. Mauri came over alone, sitting up on the bicycle and taking the newspapers for the descent. Indurain, Zülle, and Riis sprinted over the summit and took the newspapers and went down toward the valley.

The motors picked up Virenque in the town of Cauterets. He was racing through the clean neat wide white streets, drawn forward on the saddle, hands on the brake hoods, legs turning a high gear, looking up toward the mountain above the town. I knew that he was thinking about the final climb, about winning the stage, about the roar of the crowd at the finish. Cauterets was the last mountain at the head of the long valley that led to the Pont-d'Espagne; at the summit the road ran out on the high plateau, on the other side was a vast shallow valley, and the Spanish frontier.

Virenque reached Cauterets and began climbing up through the forest with the steep rock walls and white writing on the road and crowd thick as over the summit even at the bottom of the mountain. The gaps showed at 1:10 to the chase group and 4:45 to the peloton. The second motor picked up Indurain and Zülle and Riis in the valley. Riis was on the front racing to distance himself from Jalabert. Then, suddenly, Maduas was with them, and he switched to the opposite side of the road behind the team cars and attacked. Riis leaned down over the bicycle, drew himself forward on the saddle, and slowly pulled Maduas back, and they came through the town of Cauterets onto the last climb. As they rode up through the forest Riis attacked and moved clear, clawing forward, forcing, fighting on the steep road. I had not expected Riis to be so strong, not in the time trial, not in the Alps, and not in the Pyrénées, pushing the others to their limits. Indurain and Zülle instinctively stood on the pedals to chase, and then Indurain sat down with great control and forced Zülle to take the front.

The first motor showed Chiappucci, Escartin, and Buenahora climbing in a small group. The riders had all changed and many had dropped back but it was still the original break from the Peyresourde. If they caught Virenque on the plateau it would be an exciting finish. The gap came up at 1:00 to Virenque, and the motor dropped back and picked up Riis climbing alone, and then Indurain, Zülle, and Maduas. Indurain was setting the pace, Gotti came up from behind and fell back, and the three continued up the climb. I remembered the year Indurain won at Cauterets. That was before he took the Tour for the first time. Watching him climb in the yellow jersey, with his strong brown face, his features impassive like a sculpture, his body leaning forward over the bicycle, his great muscled legs turning the pedals with smooth fluid power and effortless natural grace, I was amazed at his strength, certain that he would win five Tours, and somehow sad, knowing that I was watching him at his best, and that one year he would no longer be as strong. Maybe it would come on in the high mountains, maybe it would come on one of the long flat stages, and maybe it would come in one of the smaller races, but in the end he would grow weak, the others would attack him, and he would be defeated like all champions.

Virenque had reached the high summit plateau. The road flattened and he leaned forward on the bicycle, shifted up through the gears, and began riding faster. On the right was a small green valley with rock faces and ski lifts on the far slopes, beyond were the Soulor and the Aubisque, and across the greater valley Luz Ardiden. Virenque wiped his face with his gloved hand, turned his head, and looked back over his shoulder; Pantani was not there, Chiappucci was not there, Indurain was not there. A wide smile broke over his face and he shifted into a higher gear, stood on the pedals, sprinted for a few strokes and sat down. The Festina car pulled alongside, and he slapped hands with the director and punched the air with his fist. He had attacked on the first mountain and started the break, taken the points over each of the six mountains, stayed away alone over four mountains with the chase group never more than 1:30 behind, would keep the red-and-white jersey, and was going to win the stage. It was the most beautiful ride of the Tour. Ahead the road ran out at the Pont d'Espagne and the great valley dropped away toward Spain. On the other side were the Vingemale and the Sierra de Guara leading down to Huesca and the Aragon plain and the city of Zaragoza.

Virenque came around the last corner holding up his clenched fist, and at the finish there was the roar from the French and Spanish crowd of fifty thousand. Virenque saluted once raising both arms to the crowd, saluted again kissing his hands and holding them over his head, pumped his arms and punched the air with his fists, and finally sat up on the bicycle, threw his arms wide to the sides, looked up at the sky, and crossed the line.

The red car with the Credit Lyonnais emblem and the flashing lights drove slowly over the line with two men and Jean-Marie Leblanc standing out of the roof watching silently. Virenque coasted to a stop in the Village Arrivée, and the crowd closed over him. Chiappucci and Escartin and Buenahora came in at 1:17. Riis sprinted down the straight and crossed the line at 2:29. Zülle led down the straight along the barricades, and then Indurain came around and they crossed the line at 2:34. Gotti finished at 3:25, Jalabert and Lanfranchi at 4:32, Mauri farther behind. Riis rode a good strong attacking race and took third back from Jalabert. Gotti held onto fifth. That was the overall. There was only one more mountain stage, and the places would change little now.

They showed the victory celebrations in the Village Arrivée. There was the great stage draped in yellow, the corporate banners, the commisaires, sponsors, and guests standing behind, and the podium with the two beautiful women wearing matching red Coca-Cola blouses and skirts. Virenque came onto the stage and stepped onto the podium, and the two women presented him with a clean new red-and-

white jersey with the Champion and large Festina on the front, handed
him the flowers, kissed him on both cheeks, and everybody clapped and
cheered. Between the women on the podium Virenque was smiling and
his young face was happy and excited. Only the Tour commisaires
standing behind were silent. They are the only ones who know, I
thought. Soon they will tell the riders. I wonder if they will tell them in
the team cars or back at the hotels. At least Virenque got the victory
celebration.

Once more they showed the crash on the Portet d'Aspet. In slow-
motion riders flashed past in the background. Casartelli was lying in the
sun facing the low white concrete blocks at the edge of the ravine. On
the road there was a bright red pool of blood. It is true, I thought. They
always say the Tour is more like life than anything except life itself.
Casartelli looked just like Robert lying on the boulevard below Mount
Diablo.

They cut back to Virenque climbing through the crowds, weaving
back and forth over the bicycle, his face excited, his eyes fixed on the
summit. I thought of the chapel at Ghisallo and the statue of the two
riders in the courtyard. What had the inscription said? These riders
following their dreams of glory, the light of their young existence, our
sport bitter in virtue and sweet in sacrifice. The words had sounded
wonderful that summer in Italy. Now, watching in the bar, they
sounded empty and false. Suddenly I felt an angry violent sadness and
I looked away from the television.

The victory celebrations were over. The coverage ended and I sat
alone at the bar. The show would go on. La Grande Boucle. The great
play of the Tour. It was wonderful when you saw them racing at the
front with the cheering crowds and dazzling colors and waving flags,
but the Tour was not a comedy or celebration. In the end the defeat was
always greater than the victory. The Tour was a tragedy. And all races

were the same.

It was last call in the bar. The music stopped and the bartender turned on the lights. Suddenly the bar seemed smaller and the voices were loud. People finished their drinks and began to file toward the door. Slowly the crowd thinned. I waited until I was the last person at the counter, and then I went out from the bar onto the avenue. Outside it was cold and the mist was covering the city. The avenue was deserted. I walked home in the dark.

When I reached the apartment I saw the bags in the hallway and I knew that Anne had returned. The window was open and the room was filled with cold night air. She was asleep, and I sat down on the edge of the bed. Her shoulders were rising and falling, and I could see the long slope of her body through the sheets and the profile of her face in the dark. I reached out and stroked the smooth black sheen of her hair. She had only been gone for a few days, but it felt like I had not seen her for the whole summer. I watched her for a long time, and then I undressed quietly, slipped under the sheets, wrapped my arms around her, and held her tightly as I fell asleep.

27

The next day I woke late in the morning. It was bright and sunny and there was a warm breeze coming through the window. I lay on the bed in the sun, thinking of the night before and the crowded bar and the Tour. It all seemed far away. The sheets were pushed off the bed and Anne was lying beside me. I moved close to her and kissed her on the mouth, and she opened her eyes.

"Hello," I said. She kissed me back and raised herself on her elbows. "Did you have a nice night?"

"I watched the Tour. I called you but you weren't at work. Where were you this weekend?" Anne sat up and pulled the sheets over her body.

"I should ask you the same question."

Then I remembered Friday night. I had promised to meet Anne in the city. Instead I was watching the Tour. I rolled over and sat up on the edge of the bed.

"Anne——"

"We were supposed to have dinner," she said. "I waited until I knew you weren't coming and then I went alone. I didn't want to waste the reservations."

"I came straight home and went to sleep. I was too tired to come into the city." I remembered the stage to Mende on Friday, the stage to Cauterets, and Casartelli, and Robert. Slowly the emotions of the night before returned. I stood and began to dress for a bicycle ride.

Anne watched silently as I pulled on my jersey and shorts.

"You're going for a ride? Now?"

I did not know where I would ride, but I knew that I had to be on my bicycle in the country. I had to be away from the city, away from any problems, climbing in the hot sun on the road. I looked at Anne. She was sitting against the wall with her hair down over her shoulders and her bare chest rising and falling. There were tears running down her cheeks. She brushed the hair away from her face and raised her eyes. When she spoke her voice was clear and determined.

"I won't be here when you get back." The whole year, somehow, had come to this point, removed from any bicycle race. I was poised on the brink of a decision that would affect the outcome of the year, and perhaps the course of my future. Anne had been right. I had changed. The decision was already made in my mind. For a moment I felt an overwhelming rush of sadness. Then there was the closed-off empty feeling, and I turned away, took my bicycle, and left the apartment.

When I climbed above the city the sun was high and bright and there was a strong wind blowing off the water. I stood on the pedals and swung the handlebars back and forth, sweeping around the corners and driving up the straights, with a high ringing in my ears and a tightness in my throat. As I climbed my breaths deepened, my body warmed, and I sat down and shifted gears on the long winding road. Below I could see the city glaring white, the bay stretched flat and hard in the wind, and the coastal mountains brown and hazy in the mist left over from the night before burning off now in the sun. Slowly the city and the bay grew smaller and I crested the climb and reached the ridge.

In the country there was the summer smell and the wind from the valley and I felt my body relax and my mind clear. I rode along the ridge beneath the tall blond eucalyptus and swaying pines. There was the long backslope and the rolling hills around the reservoir, and in the distance, above the valley, the tall hazy brown mass of Mount Diablo. Then I knew where I would ride. I continued south until I reached the descent, dropped through Moraga, and came out in the Diablo Valley.

On the long straight below the mountain I moved my hands to the drops and shifted into high gear. My body was tired and my legs moved mechanically. Soon I passed the place where Robert had been killed, and I turned off the boulevard onto a smaller road that led toward Mount Diablo. As you approached the mountain the view slowly changed: first you saw the massed slopes from one angle; then you turned and saw the mountain from another angle; then you turned again and there was a new view, with the summit always hidden behind and beyond what was visible. I rode through the housing developments and came out in the grassy oak country where the road began to rise into the foothills. Finally I turned onto the road that climbed to the summit of the mountain.

It was a long climb. Twelve miles. Over one hour. The resistance of the pedals increased and I slid back in the saddle and shifted down through the gears. Slowly I found a comfortable rhythm and I rounded the first corner past an oak grove. The housing developments and smooth brown foothills faded below. Now, on the mountain, I could not see the summit, and there was only the road leading upward.

Mount Diablo was not a very high mountain. In the winter there was light snow over the summit, and in the spring it was cool when you climbed above the valley, but the summit was lower than the Sierra and much lower than the Rockies. I thought of the mountains I had climbed in the United States: the long grades near Santa Cruz that came down to the ocean; the Sierra where you rode up through aspen and pine and came out above in rocky country with talus slopes and towering faces and snow-covered peaks; Mount Hood in Oregon where you rounded what looked like the summit and saw, far above, the high snow cone of the true summit; the climbs in Colorado with long steady grades and red rock and peaks so massive that you did not feel the altitude. Then there were the mountains in Europe: the climb to Asiago with the switchbacks at the bottom, the high white town of Conco, and the green alpine plateau ringed by the peaks of Mount Erio and Mount Fior; the climb from Valstagna to Foza up the narrow ravine with the steep rock walls and winding switchbacks and slender white bridge over the gorge; the Grappa, starting from the church at the bottom, past the trenches and fortifications of the old positions, to the smooth green slopes over the summit where there was a monument to the war, or the climb from the north on the narrow road that led up through a forest and came out in the open pastures that they called the Eagles' Way; finally the Passo Rolle with the long tunnels smelling of rock and water, the green valleys, the little town of Fierra de Primiero, and the road that climbed in switchbacks through red pines to the summit, where there was always snow even in the summer, and a small hotel from which you could see the Colibricon and the Gardena and the high snow-covered Dolomites crossing into Austria. But none of those climbs made you feel as high as Diablo. Diablo stood alone, rising four thousand feet straight from the floor of the valley, with only a great open expanse stretched to the horizon. On the climb you felt high and exposed and alone. They said that the view from the summit was one of widest in the world.

I came above the orchards and rounded a steep corner. On the right was a great drop, the slopes falling away to a valley covered with thrusting gray rocks. The road led up along steep tan walls, turned out of sight, came back into view rising in a straight, and disappeared over a ridge. There was no shade, the sun was directly overhead, and I could feel the dry baking heat and rising sweat on my skin. I opened my jersey and rolled up my sleeves and shorts, and then drank, poured small amounts of water over my back and shoulders, and continued climbing.

As I climbed I imagined the steady roar of the crowd and the people parting before me in two walls. I saw the cheering blurring faces and I heard the helicopter hovering overhead. I felt the rushing intensity of the Tour. Then I was back on the mountain and the road was empty and there were no cars or people in sight. I went up along the rocks walls, climbed the steep straight, and came over the ridge to the first check station. There the road flattened and I stood on the pedals to stretch my legs and rode slowly through a forest past the great yellow wind-scoured rain-eaten sandstone rock formations, coming out once more on the smooth brown open slopes and scattered with gray rocks and oak trees. Above was the thin bridge of the saddle that crossed to the higher mountain, heavy and massed, the summit still hidden from view.

From the saddle the slopes dropped on both sides, steeply at first and then more gradually, spreading down into the rolling hills and running out in the valley far below. The wind was blowing up from the valley over the ridge, and there was an open feeling with no land on the sides and only empty space. I rode onto the saddle and slowly climbed in the wind across the thin bridge of land. Then the road reached the far slopes, and I went up through the forest and reached the second check station where the south and north roads joined as one road and led toward the summit.

The road climbed gently through a pine forest with the smell of the trees and the dry red needles on the ground and the light breeze from below. Here is where you start to see snow in the winter, I thought, remembering the fresh smell of the pines in the cold air and the white snow on the ground. Then I came out from the trees and saw the climb above. The road made two steep turns and went away up the mountain. I followed the road with my eyes until I lost it in shimmering heat waves rising from the slopes. Searching, I picked up the road on the other side of the mountain, far above, showing as a faint gray line, lost the road again, and found it on the other side of the mountain, higher, almost invisible. Finally I lost the road completely, and there was only the hazy brown mountain tapering to a point against the sky that was the summit.

You never remember how long the climb is, I thought. When you pass the first check station you think you are half-way there; when you pass the second check station you think you are nearly to the summit; when you come out of the forest and see the road tracking up the mountain you know the hardest part of the climb is still ahead. I went up around the turns and reached the higher slopes. The sun was hot and there was no shade and the wind was blowing hard. My breaths were coming faster and my heart was racing and there was the deep ache in my legs. I reached down and drank and poured water over my head and shoulders. Then I leaned forward and stared at the front wheel. With the steady rhythm my thoughts began to wander and I repeated words to myself like mantras: push, push, push, keep turning the pedals, stand around the corners, pull on the handlebars, harder, harder, higher, higher, like in the Tour, like Indurain, you are on the mountain, you are alone. And then suddenly: Anne, Anne, Anne. I raised my head from the road and looked away from the mountain.

On the horizon I could see the broken line of the Sierra. Below, covered by dust, were the towns and developments in the valley. Somewhere down there Robert was killed. I thought of Casartelli and Robert. Why did I have such powerful emotions? Were my feelings directed at the circumstances? At the blind wastefulness of a young life destroyed by sport? It seemed that Casartelli was destroyed by something larger than himself, by forces that he did not understand and could not control; ambition, history, the immensity of the Tour. I felt as if my dreams were being destroyed by similar forces; time, chance, and all of the people around me who did not understand bicycle racing. Somehow Anne had become included in that crowd. She had crossed that line and stood on the other side of the barricades. To fight back I needed to be alone.

I shifted up through the gears and began climbing faster. Gradually the pain grew in my legs and spread over my body. I pushed harder, standing on the pedals and swinging the handlebars back and forth, sweeping around the corners and sprinting up the straights, my jersey open, my hair blown back, my head raised looking toward the summit. I drove myself harder, the country blurred and flowed, and the burning pain subsumed my thoughts. I was not thinking about racing, I was not thinking about Casartelli and Robert, and I was not thinking about Anne. All of the anger and sadness and confusion were driven away. There was only the high open empty feeling on the mountain.

The road to the summit climbed in steep pitches separated by switchbacks. The slopes were burned brown, and there were great ravines of broken rock and swaying gray pines. Then the pitches were shorter and the switchbacks were closer together, and I came up below the peak. Finally I reached the last pitch. The road was steep and I slowed and stood on the pedals leaning all my weight on each stroke, the heat rising from the road, the sweat running down my face, the pain shooting through my body like spears. The grade leveled and there was no higher country on the sides. I had reached the summit. I coasted slowly to the base of a small stone observation tower and slumped forward over the bicycle with my head down.

When I recovered I sat up and looked out from the mountain. Over the summit there was a steady cool wind. The sky was clear blue and in the distance were white clouds at the same level as the peak. The country spread in all directions: to the east was the Sierra; to the north was the white industrial sprawl along the upper bay and the faint outline of the Cascades; to the south was the valley basin; to the west was the country where we rode, the glint of the city and the bay, and the hazy light profile of the coastal mountains.

I took a long drink, poured water over my arms and legs to wash away the slicked sweat and salt from the climb, and ran my fingers through my hair. In the wind my skin shivered and contracted and I was cool even in the sun. I closed my jersey and rolled down my sleeves and shorts. There was still the long descent, the run home through the valley, and the climb over the ridge. I turned around in the road and started down the mountain.

28

O n July twenty-third I walked up to the bar to watch the
last stage of the Tour de France. After Cauterets I had not watched
the race. I had not seen the long funeral procession that they rode
through the Pyrénées from Tarbes to Pau, climbing slowly through
the mountains, staying together, crossing the line with no results
given at the finish, nor the stage where they came down from the
mountains to Bordeaux and began the third week of racing, nor the
stage to Limoges that Armstrong won alone and dedicated to team-
mate Casartelli, nor the final time trial at Lac de Vassiviere won by
Indurain. I did not want to think of racing except on the weekends
when I traveled to races of my own, but now, on the last day, I
wanted to watch them ride into Paris.

When I came up to the bar out of the hot noon sun it was empty
and shaded, the tables and chairs were stacked along the wall, and
there was a light breeze blowing through from the avenue. I sat down
at the counter and the bartender switched on the television. That
morning they had started out from the small town of St. Genevieve
des Bois to the south near Orleans. It was a bright summer day and
they were riding across the plain through Loiret toward Paris. The last
stage used to be a real parade. The racing was over and they rode
slowly, poured champagne into glasses from the team cars, posed for
pictures, stole hats and flags from the crowd, and sang songs. Now it

was no longer the same; they still rode slowly for the first part of the day, but there was a stage to win, and as they approached Paris they raced faster and faster, until the final fast hard laps on the Champs-Elysées.

The helicopter showed the great procession from above, and the peloton looked very small on the road. They were the riders left in the Tour. Only three weeks had passed, but it seemed like months. I was sad when I realized how many of the two-hundred-strong peloton had abandoned since St. Brieuc, when I remembered the deal-making and drug-taking in the mountains, when I thought of Casartelli and the hard-driving business behind this sport that was founded on the suffering of the riders; but there was also a feeling that they had all won, and I knew that the following year the Tour would begin again.

The motors picked up the peloton on the road. They were riding together and the jerseys formed a solid mass of bright color over the road, with the sun on their backs, all their legs cycling beneath, the country flowing past in the background, green and brown fields, bare tan and white ground, patches of yellow grass, gently rolling hills and woods, small white towns and spires showing in the distance. Indurain was riding near the front, sitting tall and straight on the bicycle, his legs turning smoothly, calm and proud in the yellow jersey. His overall time was 89:05:13. Eighty-nine hours and five minutes and thirteen seconds. Almost one hundred hours of racing over two thousand miles and twenty-three days. Zülle was second four minutes and thirty-five seconds back, and Riis was third six minutes and forty-seven seconds back. At the end of the Tour the time gaps that had seemed so great in the mountains and time trials seemed very small. Zülle had almost taken the yellow jersey. It was only his first year racing for the overall, and there was every chance that he would win in the future. Riis was the only Dane to reach the podium for many years. He was an old domestique who had turned himself into a champion, and he would not have so many chances in the future, but he had almost beaten Indurain in the first time trial, he had never stopped attacking, and with his ride in the Alps and the Pyrénées there was no reason to think that he could not reach the podium again or even win the Tour.

As they crossed the plain the motors dropped back through the peloton and found Jalabert in the green jersey and Virenque in the red-and-white jersey. Jalabert earned his fourth place, I thought. He rode into the green jersey over the stage to Mende on Bastille Day, and he handled the high mountains well. In the end he had not reached the podium, but the French could console themselves with Virenque. Virenque had the sprint to take the summit points, and his break to Cauterets was the most beautiful ride of the Tour. After the jerseys were the riders who had won stages, the riders who had made the racing, and the riders who had simply made up the peloton. And over the years they would forget the stage winners, the green and red-and-white jersey, and even those who placed second and third overall, and would only remember the winner, Miguel Indurain. He had taken his fifth Tour, and now they would always speak of him with Anquetil, Merckx, and Hinault. Indurain was one of great champions of the hundred-year history of the Tour de France.

They came toward Paris on the long straight roads over the plain, crossed under the first motorway with the people out of the cars and the crowd watching above, and approached the low white industry on the horizon. Finally they reached the outskirts of the city, and from above you could see them riding through the maze of highways and apartments and old wide tree-lined boulevards. Then the helicopter could no longer follow the race and pulled away, flying straight over the city. As the camera panned upward you saw the dark green rolling hills, and then, on the other side of the hills, the great flat dirty white spread of Paris, the tiny buildings, the diagonals of the boulevards, the winding strip of the Seine, and in the distance, taller than anything else, the soaring Eiffel Tower.

When the motors picked up the peloton they were racing through the middle of the city. In the background were crowded streets, sidewalks, open stores, cafes, metro entrances, high buildings, and the broken skyline. Banesto was working on the front, and as they came through the rotation I counted each of the riders: Rué, Aparicio, Arrieta, Marino Alonso, Thomas Davy, Aitor Garmendia, Carmelo Miranda. They were riders who had supported Indurain. They had set the pace on the flats, pulled the peloton through the mountains, made the breaks, chased the attacks, sheltered Indurain from the wind, brought him food and water, waited for him when he stopped, and rode always by his side. He could not have won the Tour without them, and they all deserved a yellow jersey. Now they would bring the peloton through Paris onto the Champs-Elysées.

The Tour reached the Seine and turned along the water. On one side there were tall green trees, and on the other the low railing, sloped bank, and many arched bridges going across to the other bank. There were barges and boats moored on the water, and the boats were crowded with people cheering and waving flags, and from the boats great plumes of water sprayed into the air. Through the rising spray, across the river, you could see the Eiffel Tower. They were racing faster, and the peloton stretched into the long line as they approached the Champs-Elysées. On the Champs-Elysées the speed was the highest of the whole Tour and nobody was ever dropped. They passed the Eiffel Tower and the Quai d'Orsay, turned away from the Seine through the Place de la Concorde, and reached the Avenue des Champs-Elysées.

The peloton and caravan turned the corner in a wide mass and they all spread out in the shimmering heat waves and thick haze on the avenue, riding away from the Place de Concorde. The Champs-Elysées ran in a long straight toward the Arc de Triomphe, split down the middle by the red-and-white barricades, with rows of tall thick green trees, vertical hanging blue-white-red French flags, and the many palaces, monuments, gardens, fountains, shops, and theaters along the avenue. Standing behind the double barricades was the crowd of a half million people. All of France and much of Europe had followed the Tour for three weeks. They had watched along the roads, in the mountains, and in the country, and now they had come to Paris to the Champs-Elysées to see the finish. When the peloton turned onto the avenue a great roar went up from the crowd, building long and sustained, with the slow swaying waving movement on the sides, and the riders came down the avenue racing toward the towering Arc de Triomphe.

It was a beautiful way to finish a bicycle race. They used to finish on the Stade Buffalo velodrome, but after they made the avenue the finishing place it seemed as if the Tour had always finished there for the last hundred years, and when I saw them come onto the Champs-Elysées with the Arc in the background, I felt a chill through my body as with the ringing of the bell on the last lap of a criterium. They would race ten laps of the Champs-Elysées. Banesto was still leading the peloton, and behind you could see the riders massing forward before the attacks that always came on the Champs-Elysées. Then the first attack went off the front, and a Castorama rider sprinted down the avenue with Virenque on his wheel. The roar of the crowd, which had not dropped since they turned onto the avenue, rose even louder, the peloton surged forward and stretched into the long line, and the two riders were caught. Banesto was no longer leading, and they reached the end of the avenue and rounded the corner at the foot of the Arc.

The line swung to the outside and leaned down and banked over the old flat worn cobbles arranged in arcs on the ground, and the riders swept through the corner and stood on the pedals and sprinted away from the Arc, racing back down the avenue toward the Place de la Concorde. When the motor picked them up there were attacks going off on the right and left. One rider pulled ahead, they showed him from the side, and I saw that it was Arturas Kasputis from the small Chazal team, crouched over the bicycle in the pink and yellow jersey, racing in the bright sun under trees, the gardens and fountains and cheering crowd behind. There were four others coming up fast and they caught Kasputis and moved clear of the peloton. The break reached the Place de la Concorde, raced across the open square where there was suddenly no crowd, swept past the fountains with the arched sprays of water, and turned onto the avenue that ran along the Seine and the Jardin de Tuileries.

The team cars and motors came up behind the break and I counted the five riders: Kasputis, Mejia, Sergei Outschakov of Polti, Flavio Vanzella of MG-Technogym, and Marco Serpellini of Lampre. They were working hard and the gap showed at twenty-eight seconds. Behind were the walls of the garden and across the river the left bank, and then they turned away from the water, dropped into a tunnel, and the motors lost them in the dark. The cameras picked them up on the other side cresting into the bright sun, and they turned and raced down the wide open Rue de Rivoli past the rows of palaces and archways and the great crowd, under the one kilometer banner, across the open Place de la Concorde, and through the sweeping corners onto the Champs-Elysées for the second lap. When they came onto the Champs-Elysées there was again the great roar from the crowd, and they raced down the avenue toward the Arc.

On the last lap the break was still ahead. The sun was lower and one side of the Champs-Elysées was cast in shadow. The break was racing down the avenue in the shadows away from the Arc. On the other side of the avenue in the bright sun you could see the peloton. Novel, Telekom, and ONCE were working on the front, and then Gewiss-Ballan, Mapei-GB, and Mercatone-Uno moved forward leading out the sprint. They reached the foot of the Arc, swung round, and came back up the avenue with the gap closing fast at thirty seconds, twenty-five seconds, twenty seconds.

The break reached the Place de la Concorde and crossed the open square and turned along the Seine. The gap showed at fifteen seconds and Outschakov attacked from behind. He had a good jump from a small group, and he had taken stage thirteen to Revel in a two-up sprint from Armstrong. Outschakov swung back and forth over the road, and the four chased behind led by Mejia. Then Mejia pulled off leaving a gap, Vanzella came through and closed the last distance, and they caught Outschakov. He ducked his head and looked back under his arm. The peloton was close behind. They turned away from the water and dropped into the tunnel, and you could see the bright jerseys in the sun as their backs lifted, and they went down into the darkness and disappeared.

When they broke out of the tunnel Outschakov was sprinting ahead of the break. Then the peloton crested from the tunnel in the long line led by Mercatone-Uno, and they came down the Rue de Rivoli and under the one kilometer banner. Vanzella was driving the break. He caught Outschakov and swung to the right, Outschakov swung to the left, and they both sat up and looked back in the road. Don't look back now, I thought, you're almost at the finish. You could see the line of the peloton snaking over the road and the riders massing forward for the sprint. Mejia dove between the two taking the front, and they reached the Place de la Concorde, raced across the open square, and swept through the last corner onto the Champs-Elysées.

The five broke onto the Champs-Elysées and the cheers erupted from the crowds. Ahead were the rows of green trees, the vertical hanging flags, the avenue shadowed on one side and bright in the sun on the other, and the long straight running to the finish and the Arc de Triomphe. It was the final break of the Tour, the last scene of the third act of the great play. The five riders led by a little climber came down the avenue, and I hoped they would stay away the same way that I hoped in the beginning and throughout the Tour that they would all make it to Paris, but I knew that they could not all win, and that they would not stay away, and that the peloton would sweep over the break for a great bunched massed sprint on the Champs-Elysées. The peloton came around the corner and spread out in the flat shimmering haze on the avenue, the front driving forward, the riders massing behind, racing toward the finish.

Who were the sprinters? There was Abdujaparov who had not yet taken a stage, Zabel who had won two stages, Jalabert who was still wearing the green jersey, Lombardi of Polti, and Martinello of Merca-tone-Uno. The finish on the Champs-Elysées was the most prestigious sprint in cycling, and all of the teams would be near the front. There were two Poltis leading the line, and they came down the barricades on the right, crossed the avenue with the line swinging behind, passed the break on the left, and dove back across the avenue toward the right. Then they were into the last five hundred meters, and you could see the 2-Sport-3 banners and red Coca-Cola boards on the sides, the blue Fiat meter markers counting down the distance to the finish, the crowd leaning over the barricades shouting and cheering and beating on the boards with their fists, and the flags of all the countries waving in the background.

At four hundred meters the first Polti began to sprint with his head down and his body low and the bicycle driving forward. At three hundred meters he swung off and dropped back, and Lombardi came through, sprinting down the middle with a Motorola, Jalabert, and Abdujaparov behind. At two hundred meters Jalabert came around Lombardi, Abdujaparov came around Jalabert, on the far left a Mercatone-Uno swung clear and began sprinting, with Museeuw, Zabel, and others who had gone on the right sprinting as well.

They came into the last hundred meters spread out across the great old Champs-Elysées sprinting for the finish of the Tour de France. Ahead you could see the red metal gantry, the red Coca-Cola banner, the Festina clock, and the ARRIVÉE growing larger, with the Arc de Triomphe in the background. In the last fifty meters Abdujaparov pulled ahead, his short body bunched over the bicycle, his legs punching down, his sharp face looking under his arm and up for the line. They came over the Fiat chevrons on the ground, the gantry spread overhead, and Abdujaparov raised his arm, clenched his fist, and swept across the line in first place. On the sides the others ducked their heads and threw their bicycles forward with a final lunge over the line.

Then it was like the finish of any other race. The peloton slowed and spread out on the Champs-Elysées, the riders stopped over their bicycles or circled back in the avenue, and you saw them standing in groups, sitting on the cobbles with their heads in their arms, and mixing with the teams and the people who spilled over the barricades on the avenue and in the Place de la Concorde. Banesto rode a victory lap of the Champs-Elysées with all the riders together, Unzue on a bicycle wearing a suit, Indurain in the middle holding a Spanish flag, and they came down the avenue with the flag streaming and flowing behind and the crowd cheering as they passed.

They showed the victory celebration on the Champs-Elysées. Now, at the end of the Tour, there was no stage draped in yellow with the backdrop of sponsors, and only a high platform and simple podium under the heavy green trees in the middle of the crowd. The ONCE team came onto the stage with Jalabert in the middle, wearing the green jersey, they were all given the yellow caps and yellow Credit Lyonnais souvenirs for the team prize, and they put on the yellow caps, held the souvenirs overhead, saluted the crowd turning first one way and then the other, and filed off the platform. Virenque came onto the platform and stepped onto the podium wearing the red-and-white jersey, and the women in the red-and-white blouses and skirts placed the can of Coca-Cola in his hand and gave him the bouquet of flowers. He held the can and flowers over his head, the women kissed him on both cheeks, the men in suits clapped, the crowd cheered, and he left the podium. Indurain, Zülle, and Riis came onto the platform. Indurain stepped onto the podium, and they presented him with the glass ornament of the Tour. Then Zülle and Riis stepped onto the podium with Indurain, they were all given flowers, they held the flowers over their heads, and there was the long sustained roar from the crowd. Finally Zülle and Riis stepped down from the podium, the French military band began to play the Spanish national anthem, and they all removed their caps and stood quietly under the trees in the bright yellow late afternoon sun listening to the drums and horns. The band stopped playing, there were last shouts and roaring cheers, and Indurain was left on the podium in the yellow jersey.

The coverage ended and I sat up at the counter. The Tour was over. The great traveling show was gone. In France the small towns would grow quiet, the paint would fade on the roads, and the

mountains would return to the glaciers and snow-covered peaks. The
Champs-Elysées would be a busy, heavily-trafficked, commercial strip
for another year. I looked away from the television. The sun had
moved overhead and there were people passing on the avenue. I
turned and went out from bar into the bright afternoon sun.

29

Along the coast it was bright and hot and the waves were crashing on the rocks and the wind was blowing off the water with the smell of the ocean. Looking down the road you could see the massed brown headlands and yellow curves of land and long sloped summer beaches against the water. The sky was clear and the sun was high over the mountains. It was August two weeks after the Tour.

In France they were racing the post-Tour criterium circuit. All through the month there were races for riders who had done well in the Tour. It was like they were amateurs, driving around the country in small cars, carrying their own bicycles, racing in one town on one day and in another town the next. The criteriums were long circuits that ran through the towns. The crowds paid to watch and the racing was all arranged by the top riders and the directors. Afterward the riders settled their contracts, got into their cars, and drove on to the next criteriums, the bigger French Cup races in Bordeaux or Paris, or the GP Quest in Plouay.

In Italy there was the Three Varese Valleys, the Coppa Agostoni, the Coppa Bernocchi, and the Tour of Veneto. In Spain there was San Sebastian, the only real summer Classic, with the climb of the Alto Jaizkibel and the finish on the Alameda del Boulevard in San Sebastian. Then the Tour of Burgos and the Tour of Galacia led up to the Vuelta a España. It was hard to believe that there was yet another great three-week tour for the year. After the Tour de France it felt like the season was over and there was nothing left.

I had not raced for weeks. John and Dave were riding together in the Pro/I-IIs and Chris was close to upgrading as well. I had not placed for the whole summer. When I rode I grew tired quickly, and I always felt like I was fighting the bicycle. Now, after the Tour, I had taken time off to recover before the fall. Beneath my fatigue I could feel my form returning. I had to find that inner core of strength that drove the best riders. In the back of my mind I knew that I was good enough race with the Pro/I-IIs. As I rode I tried to remember the times that I had raced well. In Italy the races were at least as hard as the Pro/I-II races in this country.

That summer in Italy we lived in a small hotel or albergo in the town of Paderno del Grappa at the base of the Grappa mountain. Across the road from the albergo was a converted farmhouse where we slept in rooms with hard plank floors, high overstuffed beds, washstands and wooden-shuttered windows. With the shutters closed the rooms were dark, and then in the morning or after the siesta you opened the shutters, folded them back, and there was the green and yellow plain of the Veneto, with the squares of the fields, the small towns, and the white campaniles showing over the country.

In the mornings we had fresh baked brioches and coffee in the bar of the albergo, and began training. Mondays after the races we rode slowly through the rolling hills and valleys along the base of the mountains or coasted down to the plain and rested our legs on the flats. Tuesdays we started with the ride through the Monfumo Valley in the morning, the sprints around the Montello hills, and the hard time trialing on the way back, and then motorpaced behind the team car for one hour in the afternoon. Wednesdays there was the long ride in the mountains and we climbed to Asiago or Enego or took the Grappa or the Passo Rolle, and Thursdays there was the long slow ride on the plain and we passed the old walled city of Marostica and the Palladio villas on the long straight tree-lined boulevards. Finally on Fridays before the races we rode down to the autostrada, put the bicycles in the lightest gears, and motorpaced behind the trucks driving between Treviso to Vicenza, catching the draft of the trucks and racing behind with our legs blurring fast, until we pulled off flushed and warmed in Castelfranco, rested at the cafe in the square, and came back slowly along the canals through the fields. There were races on Saturdays and Sundays making regular three-hundred-mile weeks, and when I left Italy I was in the best shape of my life.

After training we returned to the albergo, showered, dressed, and walked across the road for the midday meal. There were long benches and wooden tables with white tablecloths, pitchers of red wine, fresh baked bread, simple pasta with red sauce, and whatever meat and vegetable dishes the family that ran the albergo cooked for themselves. After the meal we crossed to the farmhouse, closed the shutters of our rooms, and rested through the heat of the day during the siesta. Then, in the afternoon, there was the second ride of the day or we watched the Tour, and then returned to the albergo for the dinners that were the same as the midday meals except that the meat and vegetable dishes changed and they did not put water in the wine. That is how we lived all summer.

Along the coast I reached the headlands and began to climb above the water. Soon the ocean was a distant flat blue and I could not hear the waves or feel the wind. Why do you always remember Italy, I wondered. Because that was the year Robert was killed. I was away in another country and all I had to do was ride my bicycle and race on the weekends. And because of Maria. Yes. Because of Maria.

In Italy every evening I borrowed a light motorcycle from the owner of the albergo and rode seven miles into Bassano to see Maria. I remembered the sun setting over the fields, the thick smell of the air, the red stone walls of the city, the wide tree-lined boulevards, and the quiet narrow streets where Maria lived. We would walk together through the squares and the old quarter to the Ponte Vecchio. After we crossed the wood-roofed bullet-marked bridge, we would follow the stone wall along the canal and drop to the bank of the Brenta River. The river was broad and shallow with wide sandbars in the middle of the stream. We would sit on the bank speaking broken English and Italian watching people pass on the bridge. At night I would ride away through Bassano, down the deserted boulevards and into the open country, the fields shining in the dark, the mountains black behind, the smell of the marshes coming across from Venice, racing through the small towns and empty squares back to the albergo.

In Europe many bicycle racers wore crosses or figures of Catholic saints around their necks. Before the races you would see them blessing the icons and making the sign of the cross. One evening in the summer, sitting on the bank of the Brenta, Maria gave me a cross on a thin gold chain. I had never been religious, but I wore the cross all summer. When I rode the cross lay beneath my jersey against my chest, and when I climbed the cross fell away from the open collar of my jersey and swung back and forth in the sun. Through July and August I won four cups in the races. Finally I placed in the top three and gave the flowers to Maria.

At the end of the summer I drove into Bassano to see Maria. I was leaving Veneto the next day and I knew that I would never see her again. We walked to the Ponte Vecchio, crossed the bridge, and followed the stone wall along the canal. Before we dropped to the river bank I took off the cross and gave it back to Maria. As I placed the cross in her hand it slipped between her fingers and fell into the sluiceway that was running high and fast from the late summer storms. We both got down on our hands and knees, and I reached into the canal up to my shoulder, but the water was pushing up against the iron bars of the grate, and the cross was gone. We sat on the bank and watched the mountains slowly grow dark as the water flowed past in the river.

I came over the crest of the headlands and dropped in a long building rush toward the coast, leaning down in a low tuck, sweeping through the corners, running out along the flats. The road led into the dunes, dry and white and sculpted by the wind. Then the road came back into the grassy brown hills, with bare fields on the sides, tall swaying eucalyptus in rows, and stands of pines and cypress that were red in the summer.

This is the where you came with Anne in the spring, I remembered. She drove out to the coast and you motorpaced behind the car and walked down to the beach. It seemed like a long time ago. I loved her then. I still loved her. Sometimes when I came home from bicycle rides, or when I woke up in the morning, I imagined her bag in the hallway, her clothes on the floor, her beautiful face and bright smile and laugh. She had left. She did not leave, I corrected myself, you are the one who left. But that did not matter. She was gone. It was the same as with Maria. Anne and I did not live in separate countries, but I knew that I would never see her again.

The road came out in the fields and there was a long straight leading toward Santa Cruz. The sun was lower on the horizon and the wind backed around to the south. I knew that soon the bank's mist would come off the water making the light hazy and soft, and that the mist would close cold and gray over the road. I could follow one of the long steady grades up into the mountains, or turn around and ride back up the coast the way I had come. It did not really matter. The distances were the same and it was all good training. I only needed one more place to upgrade to Pro/I-II. You can do it, I told myself. You have placed many times in the past. You have to place. Time is running out. Soon it will be fall. But the season was not over yet.

30

The last road race of the year was held in the Great Central Valley. We started out in the hills to the west, came down into the valley, and turned onto the long straight roads through the fields. The sun was baking hot and the wind blowing over the fields raising the dust and making your eyes and throat burn. I was riding in the middle of the pack with my jersey open and my shorts and sleeves rolled up in the sun. There were only a few riders left in the pack. We moved off down the road in a slow winding procession.

An early break went clear and the pack began to chase. We stretched into a long line and I leaned down over the bicycle and shifted up through the gears. Right away I began to fall back through the pack. The race had not even started and already I was getting dropped. It was too fast. I had been riding long distances but my body was not accustomed to the speed. Eighty miles. Four hours. I knew I would never stay with the pack. Just hold on, I thought. Hold onto the wheel in front of you. Maybe you will come around for the finish. If you stay with the pack you can place in the sprint.

When we came through the feedzone on the fourth lap I was riding in the middle of the line. My legs were weak and my body was empty and beyond-sweating in the heat. I had finished all of my water and I threw the empty bottles away and moved to front. Ahead was the long straight with the people standing in rows and the banner and the finish in the background. We swept into the feedzone with the sudden cheers and shouts and people running alongside, and a bottle slapped heavy and full into my outstretched hand. Quickly I placed the bottle on my frame and looked up for another, but we were already past and the sounds faded behind.

We began the last lap of the road race. The break was caught and riders began to attack. Every time there was an attack the front surged and the speed climbed higher. The country flattened into a streaming blur, and I shifted into the highest gear and held the wheel ahead. At the front they kept attacking.

The pack surged and the speed climbed and the wheel ahead pulled away. As the gap opened the wind came up hard and there was a high roaring sound and heavy resistance on the pedals, and I lost the wheel ahead. Slowly I drew myself back into the draft, fighting forward for every inch, my legs suddenly alive with pain. Again the pack surged, the wheel pulled away, and the gap opened on the road. Riders sprinted past on both sides and I fell back. Get on a wheel, I yelled to myself. Get on a wheel or you are going to be dropped. I sprinted into the wind and sat down and narrowed my body in the smooth silent rush of the draft. Ducking my head I looked back under my arm. There was the end of the line and the caravan following slowly behind. The caravan was clearly visible and I could see the empty road in the background. Don't look back again, I thought. You are too close. I turned around and stared at the wheel ahead.

The pack surged and the wheel pulled away and the gap opened on the road. The wind came up and I dropped back. Riders sprinted past on both sides and could feel myself drawing near the end of the line. When the last rider came around and I jumped on the pedals and sprinted desperately for his wheel. The pain overwhelmed my body and I sat down heavily. The rider was so close that I could have reached out and touched him, but I could not ride any faster. There was no way to close the gap. I held the gap constant for as long as I could, and then, slowly, the last rider pulled away. The gap opened from one bicycle length to two, then three, then four, and finally I was dropped from the end of the line.

The caravan came around with the loud revving of the car engines and I dove across the road into the draft. For a moment there was a draw of speed, and then the cars pulled away and I was alone. There was only the high sound of the wind and my breaths heaving in my chest. I looked back and saw the long straight road with the flat bare fields on the sides and the dust rising in swirling clouds. There were no other groups behind and I turned back around. The pack slowly receded in the shimmering heat waves on the road.

They dropped you, I thought. They dropped you in the last road race of the season. I looked down at my legs, burned brown from the sun, streaked with sweat and dust, still turning a high gear. Again they were not strong enough. Again I had failed. But I had to keep riding. I could not stop. Maybe I would catch the pack.

I rode through the valley with my head down and my hands in the drops and my legs turning mechanically. Every few miles I shifted position, reached down to drink, or poured a small amount of water over my back and shoulders. Slowly my head dropped lower and my hands became numb and I lost the feeling in my legs. When my head almost touched the handlebars I jerked my body upright and straightened my arms and stood on the pedals for a few strokes before settling back into the steady pace. You don't have to keep riding, I thought. You can stop and wait for the caravan. They will take you back to the finish. I knew then that I would not catch the pack, but I did not want to drop out of the race. There was a difference between getting dropped and dropping out of a race. Remember that, I told myself. You have not dropped out yet, and you will not give up until you reach the finish. It was like a long time trial with no end. You had to keep going and you could not stop. But I did not know how much longer I could continue.

I drank the last of my water and let the bottle blow away behind. In the distance heat waves shimmered like mirages. Suddenly I realized that I was coasting with one leg extended and the other bent at the top of the stroke. Quickly I resumed pedaling and shifted into a lighter gear to keep my legs moving. I did not want my legs to cramp. Then I was coasting again and I slowed down on the road. I kept going, pedaling and coasting, pedaling and coasting, riding slower and slower, until I was weaving back and forth and only the bicycle was holding me upright.

Finally I stopped by the side of the road and unclipped from the pedals. I leaned forward over the bicycle and rested my head on the handlebars. I was finished. I had gone deep into my reserves and I had nothing left. The race was over. An overwhelming feeling of defeat moved through me in waves, but I was too tired to care about the race. Eventually I stood up and looked around at the country. The sun was directly overhead and there were a few high white clouds moving away toward the coast. In the distance I could see the faint outline of the hills. I had come all the way back around the course. I had almost made it. The finish was close. I knew that I had to get back to the cars. I clipped into the pedals and rode slowly down the valley toward the hills.

31

I n late September there was a three-day storm. The clouds came off the ocean from the north, and there were strong winds and intermittent rain for three days before the storm moved away. For several days afterward the wind did not drop, and there were heavy swells along the coast and new green grass over the hills and the flowers that came with the rains. Finally the winds changed, blowing from inland, the hills turned brown again, and there was the sharp dry feeling in the air and the hottest days of the year. I knew the inland wind meant that it was growing cold in the mountains, and that the cold air was dropping from the Sierra, warming and drying across the valley, and pushing out to sea through the breaks in the coastal range. It would be winter soon. In the foothills the aspen were turning yellow and gold, the air was crisp and cold, and with the rain there was the first snow at higher elevations.

On one of the long fall evenings I rode into the hills above the city. It was warm and I opened my jersey and rolled up my sleeves and shorts in the sun. Below I could see the city and the bay, and across the water San Francisco and the mountains at the coast. I climbed higher and rode over the ridge into the parks.

When I came over the ridge there was a hot wind and the sharp dry smell of the country. I shifted up through the gears and leaned forward over the bicycle holding a steady pace. Looking down through the trees

I could see the brown slopes with the high grass moving in waves, the stands of eucalyptus and pine swaying in the wind, and the smooth rolling hills. The country looked much like that of winter, but it was not the same. When I looked at the country in the winter there was hope and promise for the coming year. Now the season was over, and when I looked at the country there was only a feeling of failure.

How had I ever convinced myself that I could upgrade to Pro/I-II? I was not a very good bicycle racer. I knew how get to the front in the criteriums, I knew how to hold my position, and I knew how to place in the sprints, but criteriums were not real races, not like the long road races that made the season and Classics in Europe. I did not even have a very good sprint. That is why I did not win more often. I was lucky to win that one race.

Oh, that's not true, I thought. Criteriums are races like any other. I was a good sprinter, and I had always done my best. I placed in most of the criteriums I entered, and I won several races over the years. That was something many riders would be happy to have accomplished. I was just not good enough to make it at the end of the year.

Why had I chosen bicycle racing? There were many other sports that were not difficult, many other sports where you never pushed yourself to your limits. In bicycle racing there was always a point where you reached the boundary of your physical and mental abilities. That was why it was so hard. The points and categories were just numbers. They did not tell the whole truth or story of the race, and I had done much with bicycle racing over the years. There were many more years ahead and I could always keep racing.

Sometimes I did not know if I even wanted to upgrade. The racing was much faster, the training was much harder, and I would not be able to think of winning. You did not race against the professionals so much as race against yourself. I knew that I could place in the smaller criteriums in the middle of the season when most of the professionals were away racing the national calendar events, but I did not know if the races in the Great Central Valley in the summer were worth all the work it would take to upgrade. And when I remembered the Tour and the darker side of the sport I no longer wanted to race at all. There were many reasons why I loved bicycle riding that had nothing to do with racing; the freedom on the road, the connection to the country; the community of friends.

I told myself these things over and over, but when I thought about the season there was still a cold resolute feeling of failure in my mind. I had wanted to upgrade more than anything, and I had not succeeded. My dreams had been destroyed. You had a wonderful spring, I thought, but in the summer you lost everything. You should have stopped after you won that race. You should have stopped in the spring. I was left with the memory of walking home with Anne after I had won the Berkeley criterium.

The fall semester had begun and I was back in college. Days in Berkeley were again filled with classes, study sessions, exams, and parties. Slowly I returned to everyday life from the world of bicycle racing. I told myself that I was still the same twenty-two-year-old young man with many opportunities for the future. I did not matter that I had not upgraded. In the end bicycle racing was just a sport. I still did not know what I would do the following year, but I had the winter and spring to decide before I graduated.

The road came out from the trees along the ridge and I began the long descent into the country. Leaning over the bicycle I felt the wind build as I gained speed, and I went down under the trees and through the fast curves dropping on the descent. When I came out below I turned along the highway and reached the climb that led toward Moraga. It was shaded under the trees and I stood on the pedals and climbed through the flickering sun and shade.

In Europe the Vuelta a España was over. They started with the prologue in Zaragoza and rode west through Navarre to La Coruna on the Atlantic coast. The first time trial was in Salamanca, and there was the stage through the rocky Sierra de Gredos to Avila, the run south to Cordoba and Seville in Andalucia, and the stages leading north and west through the Sierra Nevada to Valencia on the Mediterranean coast. Then they came up the coast to Barcelona for the circuit race, and rode into the Pyrénées to Luz Ardiden. Finally they left the mountains for the last time trial in Alcala de Henares and the finish in Madrid. The Vuelta used to be held in the spring. Now it was a hard race at the end of the season with the heat and distance and mountains.

Jalabert won the jersey de oro. He took the stages to Alto de Naranco, Orense, Avila, Barcelona, and Luz Ardiden, and would have won at Sierra Nevada as well had he not offered the stage to a domestique from a smaller team for a strong ride in the mountains. They loved him even more for that in Spain; Jalabert was always considered a little more Spanish than French, and they had given him the official Catalan name of Gelebert. Zülle won the stage to Pla de Beret, and the Spaniard Abraham Olano took the prologue in Zaragoza and the time trials in Salamanca and Alcala de Henares. They said that Olano would have won the Vuelta overall if Jalabert had not been so strong in the mountains.

In France there was the Tour de l'Avenir. They called it the Tour of the Future because it was only for young espoir professionals and amateurs. The race crossed the Alps and for many riders it was their first experience in the high mountains. Those who showed well at the Tour de l'Avenir often went on to become good professionals. A young Frenchman had won. Perhaps they had found a new champion.

After the Tour de l'Avenir there was Paris-Brussels, the GP

Fourmies, and the GP d'Isbergues in France, and Milan-Vignola, the Tour of Romagna, the Tour of Lazio, the Tour of Emilia, the Coppa Placci, and the Coppa Sabatini in Italy. These races made the series of semi-Classics leading up to the world championships.

Worlds were in Colombia. Every year the race changed from country to country. They raced on national teams and there were always rivalries between countries and alliances between riders who were on trade teams for most of the season. It was only a one-day race, and sometimes there were surprise winners, but usually the course was hard enough to force a selection and you only saw true champions at the finish. The winner took the pure white jersey with the band of blue, red, black, yellow, and green stripes across the chest. In France they called it the *maillot arc-en-ciel* or rainbow jersey. In Italy they called it the *maglia sognata* or jersey of dreams. The world champion wore the jersey all through the following year until the next championship, and was thereafter entitled to wear the stripes on the sleeves and collar of his jersey for the rest of his career to show that he had once been world champion. Some people said that the jersey was a curse because of the long runs of bad luck that often followed world champions, but all of the riders in the peloton still wanted to wear the *maglia sognata*.

It was strange to have Worlds in South America. The race was in the mountains in the north near Bogota. They would start in the town of Duitama and climb to Santa Luca. They said that all the roads in the mountains were dirt and that the government was paving them especially for the race. I knew it would be hard with the long journey from Europe, the foreign culture, and the high altitude. Maybe one of the Colombians would win. It would be wonderful to see Muñoz or Buenahora take the jersey in their own country.

After Worlds there were smaller races like the Subida al Naranco in

Spain and Paris-Bourges in France, and then the fall Classic. The fall
Classics started with Paris-Tours, where you always saw the peloton
coming down the long straight roads bordered by rows of white plane
trees, the sun pale and bright, riders wearing arm-warmers and gloves
in the cool fall weather. The race was flat and very fast and usually
finished in a sprint on the wide open Avenue de Grammont. In Italy
there was Milan-Turin, the Tour of Piedmont, and finally the Tour of
Lombardy. The Tour of Lombardy was the last Classic before the end
of the year.

It was a long season. There was no other sport with events of real
importance from February to October. And with the Six Day races on
the indoor tracks in the winter, all of the new races opening the markets
in Japan, China, and Malaysia, and the races in Mexico, Australia, and
South Africa, there was really no break in the year.

I came over the crest of the hill above Moraga. Below I could see the
houses of the town and the canyons leading back toward the ridge. I
dropped on the long grade and reached the last climb. When I rode
from the bright sun of the valley into the forest I was blinded for a
moment in the dark. Then my eyes adjusted and I saw the great trees
with the light filtering down through the tops, the heavy growth
below, and the leaves dusty and gray. Coming into the open around the
first steep corner I saw the backslope of the hills cast in shadow. In the
distance was Mount Diablo, tall and uplifted, with the summit shining
in the sun, and far across the valley the faint line of the Sierra with the
first snow over the peaks.

The road climbed toward the ridge. I shifted up through the gears
and began riding faster. I was not fighting the bicycle and my legs
moved with natural flowing rhythm. The road turned and turned
again, growing steeper near the ridge. Finally I reached the last steep
pitch and came over the crest.

I rode from the shade of the climb into the warm glow of the setting sun. The tall buildings of San Francisco were glinting in the light, the clouds were edged with color, and the mountains were black along the coast. The sun was burning long and deep and red over the ocean. I started down toward the city.

32

The last criterium of the year was held in San Francisco. It was a bright sunny fall day. As I crossed the bridge I could see the bay chopped into whitecaps, sailboats dotting the water, and the tall buildings of San Francisco outlined against the blue sky. I came down into the city, drove through downtown, and reached the course.

The criterium ran between the old brick warehouses and parks near the water. The streets were blocked with barricades, there was an official platform and announcing stand, and a large crowd gathered at the finish. The Category IV race was underway. I changed into my race clothing and rode away from the course on the Embarcadero. Along the waterfront the the air was cool and smelled of the ocean. Looking back across the bay I could see the white flats of Berkeley and the hills where we rode.

The season was almost over. Olano won the maglia sognata at the world championships. I did not think that he was that strong, but he came out of the Vuelta with good form, made the final break in Duitama, and attacked in the rain on the last lap to finish alone. Indurain came in second and Spain took the first two places. Olano and Indurain were both from Navarre, and on the podium they looked like brothers, with the same Basque face, black hair, and dark eyes. Now they were racing the fall Classics.

Olano won the Subida al Naranco showing the rainbow jersey for the first time. A young Italian won Paris-Tours in a bunch sprint on the Avenue de Grammont. A young Belgian won Paris-Brussels. Chiappucci took the Tour of Piedmont. Museeuw was leading the World Cup. There was only one classic left, the Tour of Lombardy.

I thought of them racing through Lombardy and along Lake Como, the sun low and bright on the water, the steep green slopes rising to the Ghisallo chapel, the Dolomites in the background. It would be cool if the wind came down from Switzerland where it snowed in the high mountains.

After Lombardy there was the Escalada Montjuich in Spain. On the same day they held an uphill time trial and a circuit race through old Montjuich park in Barcelona. Then the year was over. There were other races in the fall, but Montjuich was the last real race of the European season. You never realized that the season had finished until winter. Then suddenly there was the GP d'Ouverture La Marseillaise in the spring, and another season began.

Along the Embarcadero I leaned down over the bicycle and began riding faster. Slowly my breaths deepened and my body warmed. I worked through the gears, drawing myself forward on the saddle until my legs were spinning fast and smooth and my body was covered with a light sweat. When I reached the end of the Embarcadero I turned around and rode slowly back to the course.

The pack was staging under the banner. I pushed through the crowd and ducked under the barricades. The crowd was watching from the sides, there was music playing, and the others were talking and laughing. Out of the four I was the last rider left from the start of the year. John had upgraded, Dave had upgraded, and Chris had stopped after the last road race. I still needed one more placing to upgrade to the Pro/I-IIs. I had not been riding for several weeks, but I had nothing to lose. I would take my chance, race the last criterium, and stop for the year.

When the pack gathered the riders grew silent and the official walked into the road to read the race directions. There were fifty laps, lap cards showed with ten to go, and free laps stopped at five. The official cleared the course and raised the starting pistol. I clipped into the pedals and slid back in the saddle, looking ahead down the wide empty straight toward the first corner white in the sun. Then I heard the sharp report of the pistol, the crowd cheered, and I pushed down and rolled forward with the others. We sprinted away from the line, spread out before the first corner, and turned onto the hill.

The colorful swaying mass of the pack moved up the hill. There were over one hundred riders. We funneled into the high cresting corner and turned onto the downhill. Slowly the pack stretched into line, and I leaned forward over the bicycle and shifted up through the gears with the smooth building wind. Before the downhill corner the line swung to the outside, and without braking we banked over the road, raced through the corner in a hurtling rush, came upright for a moment on the short straight, and dove into the final corner.

I looked down the straight. The road was bordered by heavy green trees that formed a long shaded tunnel. Far ahead, where the trees lifted away, I could see the crowd and the banner in the sun. We raced down the straight under the trees, broke into the sun, and swept past the finish with the crowd cheering and the announcer shouting and the music playing. The first riders attacked, and behind, in the middle of the pack, I watched the break move clear, wondering if we would see them again before the finish.

With five to go the break had been caught and the pack was all together. I was riding at the front and the feeling of summer was gone. My legs felt strong and my movements were smooth and fluid and my mind was clear and focused. I realized that it was one of the days when I could win.

We turned onto the hill and I stood on the pedals climbing fast out of the saddle in the tight bunched pack. The front crested the hill and slowed in the corner. Suddenly there were shouts and squealing brakes and building sounds of a crash, and I saw bicycles and riders falling on the straight. The line was driving up the hill and I was trapped in the middle of the pack. No, I thought. You can't crash now. Not with five laps to go in the last race of the year.

The crash moved through the pack and I leaned hard and pushed against the rider on the outside. We were almost past when I saw that we were not going to make it and I braked hard and braced myself with the inward tensing fear. Something hit my thigh hard and my pedal came down on the ground lifting the rear wheel. I unclipped one foot as the bicycle slid across the straight. We came up fast on the barricades and the rider beside me crashed and went over sideways. I rounded the corner and came upright slowed almost to a stop on the downhill.

I clipped into the pedals and stood on the gear bringing the bicycle back up to speed. You made it past the crash, I thought. It's all behind you. Now you have to get back to the front. Looking ahead I saw the pack stretched into a long line, broken apart after the crash, with a small front group rounding the far corner.

I raced toward the end of the line. When I reached the last rider I came up through the draft and sprinted past. There was a group ahead, and I went straight through the group, dove into the downhill corner, and turned onto the straight. I went up the line, sprinting from rider to rider, group to group, not feeling the pedals, not feeling the pain in my legs, thinking only of the finish.

With two laps to go I fought back to the front group. On the downhill I drew onto the last wheel and sat up and coasted, breathing hard, my heart pounding, my legs flushed with pain from the chase. There were two more laps before the sprint. I was back in the race. I reached down and drank the last of my water, and then I leaned forward and went up through the rotation toward the front.

On the last lap we swept past the finish with the crowd cheering and the announcer shouting and the music playing, and over the roar of the crowd I heard the high ringing of the bell. I was at the front, the sides were open, and the straight was clear ahead. I dove into the first corner and came up the hill climbing fast out of the saddle. My body was working over the bicycle, my breaths were deep and full, and all the fatigue was gone with the building excitement of the sprint. I crested the hill and pulled to the side, and the others came under me in a driving line. I dropped onto the last wheel and we turned onto the downhill.

On the downhill I tucked low in the rushing wind. God it's fast, I thought. Turning my head I looked back over my shoulder. The sound of the wind subsided, and in the silence of the draft I saw the pack stretched into a long single line. At the front we formed a small break, and I knew that if we kept the speed high we could stay away to the finish. I went up through the rotation and pulled hard and dropped back, and we reached the last two turns. The line swung to the outside and banked over the road, and traveling impossibly fast we raced through the corner, came upright on the short straight, and dove into the final corner.

We swept onto the long straight and I immediately looked up and counted the riders ahead. I was in eighth position. Ducking my head I looked back under my arm and saw the pack round the final corner and spread out in a flat haze on the straight. They were chasing hard. We still had a small gap and there was a chance we would make it. Far ahead, down the long tunnel of trees, I could see the finish in the bright sun. The group flattened into line in the gutter and the first rider began to lead out the sprint. I shifted up through the gears, feeling the chain drop down, as we raced through the shade under the trees.

The first rider slowed and dropped back, and we swept past in a driving line. Then the second rider took over the lead, moving across the straight with the line snaking behind. Don't go too early, I told myself. Wait until you can see the banner. Wait until you are sure you will place in the sprint. The second rider slowed and dropped back, and the others came around sprinting hard with their heads down and the bicycles going from side to side. I followed the line to the right, and then I could see the finish clearly, with the banner above and the people on the sides leaning into the road looking down the straight. Now, I thought. Yes, now. I dropped back from the wheel ahead, shifted into the highest gear, and jumped on the pedals. I sprinted up through the draft, and at the last moment I swung away and came around into the open.

When I came around there was the sudden roar of wind and the heavy resistance of the gear, and I drove forward throwing the handlebars back and forth leaning all my weight on each stroke. Gradually the gear came over with the building momentum and fast rhythm of the sprint, and I moved toward the center of the road. Ahead was one rider on the right and three on the left. I drew even with the last rider and we raced shoulder to shoulder close to the barricades. Then I pulled ahead, and he faded behind and disappeared.

You are in fourth place, I thought. The pack will not mass forward now. Nobody will suddenly sprint past. There will be no more crashes. You are going to place. When I realized that I was going to place I was filled with sudden elated happiness. All year I had worked hard, I had not stopped when it was difficult, and I had kept racing even when I thought that I had no chance. I remembered the first ride in the winter, all of the work on the bicycle, all the miles on the road, and all the races in the spring and summer. Finally my dream had come true. I was going to race with the Pro/I-IIs.

The desperate drive of the race faded and I was overcome with relieved satisfaction as after a long ride. In the back of my mind there was also a hardened understanding of the hollow rewards of success at great cost. I knew that the race was not over. In fact, the race had only just begun. The following year would be as difficult or more so than the year that had passed. However, I was happy to have succeeded in the old, colorful, beautiful, wonderful sport I loved.

We came out from the tunnel of trees into the bright sun and there was the roar from the crowd and the slow swaying waving motion along the straight. The announcer was shouting and the crowd was cheering and ahead was the finish. I was drawn forward over the front wheel, my breaths heaving, my heart pounding, my legs driving down. Looking up I saw the banner spreading over the straight, and I gathered my body over the bicycle, bent my arms and legs, dropped my head, and threw my bicycle forward over the line.

Other cycling books from BREAKAWAY

NORTH WIND IN YOUR SPOKES: A Novel of the Tour de France, by Hans Blickensdorfer $23, hardcover, 1-891369-18-0 / $13, paperback, ISBN: 1-891369-39-3 "Here it is—the great sports novel. It couldn't get any more exciting." *–The World*

THE YELLOW JERSEY, by Ralph Hurne. 285 pages, paperback, $14.95. ISBN: 1-55821-452-6   "The greatest cycling novel ever written." *—Bicycling.*

BECOMING AN IRONMAN: First Encounters With the Ultimate Endurance Event. Edited by Kara Douglass Thom. Personal stories of athletes' first Ironman. 288 pages. Hardcover, $23, ISBN: 1-891369-24-5. Paperback, $14, ISBN: 1-891369-31-8

METAL COWBOY: Tales from the Road Less Pedaled, by Joe Kurmaskie. 304 pages, $23.00, hardcover, ISBN: 1-891369-10-5. "An incredibly entertaining, vivid account of the people met and experiences collected during his trips bicycling around the world." *—Foreword*

THE QUOTABLE CYCLIST: Great Moments of Bicycling Wisdom, Inspiration, and Humor. Edited by Bill Strickland. 360 pages. Hardcover, $22, ISBN: 1-55821-563-8. Paperback, $13, ISBN: 1-891369-27-X. A splendid collection of quotes about all aspects of bikes.

SPOKESONGS: Bicycle Adventures on Three Continents, by Willie Weir $21, hardcover, 1-891369-17-2. An intrepid cyclist sees the world and writes beautifully (and humorously) about it.

THE WHEELS OF CHANCE: A Bicycling Idyll, by H. G. Wells. Classic 1896 cycling novel—funny, pastoral, dramatic, and romantic—by renowned author. Delirious good fun, and good literature. 284 pages, paperback, $12.95. ISBN: 1-55821-564-6

IN BOOKSTORES EVERYWHERE,
OR DIRECTLY FROM BREAKAWAY BOOKS.
www.breakawaybooks.com   (800) 548-4348